Maximize Your SUPER POWERS

Vol. 1

Capri Cruz, PhD

www.CapriCruz.com

Contents

Dedication

To my unborn grandchildren and their angelic mother: The thought of you is my superpower.

To my beloved brother:
I owe everything to you.

Dear younger self,

I think of you often, and I smile. You were such a precious little thing. I often wonder what it would be like to meet you today. Do you think we can just sit and talk for a moment? When I see your face, my heart pains because I know of so much that you had to go through just so I could be here today, and yet, I know that I know so very little. I just can't imagine what it was like for you at 3, 7, 9, 11, and 15 years old. You endured so much pain and tragedy so early in life; it boggles my mind how you were able to stay safe for so long. Words are insufficient to describe my admiration for you.

There's so much more I want to say to you; where should I start? I guess I'll start with I'm sorry.

I'm sorry I wasn't there to help you. I'm sorry no one was there to help you. You didn't deserve anything, anything at all that you went through; please know none of it was your fault. The people who were supposed to care, protect, and love you, failed. They failed horribly and you suffer for it. I can't imagine how confused you were as a child bouncing around from one stranger's home to another, never knowing if you were going to get beaten, sexually violated, or suffocated again. The fear that must have consumed your mind, my God, I am so sorry baby.

You did not deserve for your parents to fail you. You did not deserve for your family to abandon you. You actually deserved to be raised by loving, functional, and healthy parents in a safe environment so you could grown up with a strong sense of identity, esteem, value, and purpose. You deserved a family to fight for you. You did not deserve to grow up petrified and alone.

I can't imagine what it took for a little girl like you to survive growing up without any family during the most vulnerable years of your life, while being beaten, molested, and demeaned by people not worthy of the oxygen they

*breathed. I am in awe of you. I am in awe of your ability to
persevere. I know you were surrounded by very scary people
your entire childhood, subjected to their evil, their harm,
their neglect, and their abandonment, and yet, deep down I
have to believe they had no idea that they were so
diabolically dysfunctional because who would knowingly be
evil and hurt someone as precious as you?*

*How did you survive it all? How did you protect yourself
when they beat you, molested you, and carelessly kicked you
out of their homes? Where does an abandoned child go
when she has nowhere to go? How did you endure the
dangerous streets of New York City as a homeless teenager?
How did you outlive never being loved?*

*You are my hero because you survived it all. It's no
wonder that by 15 you became a runaway. I suppose that's
the exact reason so many other teens runaway; they just
want to get away from those who are hurting them, but
rarely do they ever have anywhere safe to go. No one will*

ever understand what you had to overcome, so don't expect them to. You alone must learn how to transmute your pain into power. It's an incredibly daunting conundrum but you will grow to learn that it's all for purpose.

The price you had to pay will never be recouped, and still, your heart must go on.

Much time had to pass before ever getting your life in order because you lacked a blueprint in life to follow, but by God girl, I want you to know you did it! You fucking did it! Those sons-of-bitches tried their best to take you out, and not only did you not die, you overcame and superseded them. To God be the glory! You are my hero, little girl – Thank you for keeping us safe long enough for me to surface. However you managed to sustain, I want you to know that you won. You won girl and you won big! Yeah, you did.

You won because you learned how to tap into your superpowers. You learned to care for yourself, you found the secret to happiness, you awakened to creation and contribution for society, and you evolved into the kind of human being who prays for those who, try as they might, were never able to kill your spirit. You did not let them harden your heart. You learned how to forgive, and in turn, was rewarded with remarkable blessings: inner peace and vision. You became a spiritual alchemist.

Despite all you suffered, I want you to know that you grew up to be an incredible woman whose emotional scars now save people's lives. Everyday when you wake up, your new mentality is that you are just getting started and that philosophy fuels your approach to life's ingenuity. You don't look back unless there's a lesson to learn from it. Instead, you seek the next best way to accomplish the mission; the mission being your greatness. You are truly phenomenal! However you survived all those years scared, alone, and in danger, I want to thank you. You did your job longer than you should have, but today I want you to know that now I take care of us.

One day I woke up in a fiery and decided we deserved a better life. I will not lie, it has been the fight of my life, but nothing compared to the fight you endured as a child. Still, I had to dig deep into the darkness of your mind so that I could create a new mind. I had to retrain our brain, create new neural circuitry, and find the next version of the little girl who hid so far inside herself she almost jeopardized my ability to elevate. No easy task, I assure you. I had to unlearn everything that you learned, which kept you safe, so that I could relearn it all again smartly. I realized that what once served you now hindered me. Thirty-seven years of chains that bounded us had to be broken. I had to learn how to step into my personal power despite never knowing I had any. As time ticked on I learned how to turn that personal power into superpowers. I learned how to make miracles happen for us.

Thank you for all you did to keep us safe. Now, watch me work!

Love your older self,

DESIGN YOUR DESTINY
with Dr. Cruz

Dear older self,

We have risen like the Phoenix.

Let's fly!

Love your keeper,

1

<u>Superpowers – What Are They?</u>

"I discovered that my insecurities and flaws were things that I actually needed to embrace, so I let them become my superpowers."

~ Skylar Grey

As humans, you and I are not vastly different. We all have the same biological building blocks that have created us to become this living, breathing specimen that seeks to survive. We are all created from atoms, molecules, and cells; we all have organs such as a heart, brain, and lungs; and we all have the same basic needs that must be met if we are to achieve the first level of existence: the need for oxygen, to feel loved, safe, valued, and fed. But here is where most of our commonalities seem to end.

Maybe like you, I've journeyed what seems to be a million miles on a path of continual evolution unknowingly becoming the person I am to ultimately become. Through each stage of evolution I've been able to advance in life first by the Grace of God, and secondly, by this incredible and often times elusive awakening to greater awareness and my ability to assimilate that awareness into a new and different stage of evolution. Here is where the evolution of who you become and who I become gets tricky. Awareness. What is it and how do we get the needed awareness at the proper time for our continued development as evolving beings?

As I look back on my life, each personal shift occurred when I was able to awaken to my internal experiences as they related to that which I was being exposed to in any given moment and my ability to assimilate the content of my awareness into an understanding of my own being in that moment. The more awareness I could awaken to the more awakened I was to my reality. You see, we are limited in our perspectives when we are limited in our awareness and the ability to assimilate that awareness.

Awaken Internally

The clearer I became of my mental reality due to this ever increasing awareness, the better able I was to intuitively know when I was in or out of alignment with that which was best for me. My spirit, I have found, has always been my guide; I just did not know how to access it in order to benefit from its insight because I was so busy looking outside of myself for answers from people who had no idea what was best for me. For decades I didn't know to ask, "Who am I and what am I supposed to be doing with my life", but once I did, it became the gateway to self-knowledge.

When I learned how to pay attention to what was being revealed to me, my awareness increased, and step-by-step, a more ideal path presented itself. Once I became aware of what I became aware of in any given moment, I realized its purpose of serving me no longer served me. The revelation of it into my awareness was indication that I needed to grow from it and use it as a springboard to greater evolution. Most people like to hold on to the old; it's familiar. It might be all we know but when I realized my life was calling me, my spirit would not let me get away with being complacent. It created an internal struggle. I would either find courage to evolve or I would suffer.

As I journeyed into new paths of life, I became awakened to those who had gone before me, observing the paths they had taken. This can be a very rich form of education if we can objectively analyze and control our emotions. Regret, fear, and jealousy do not serve us except to learn and grow from them. Our egos often try to keep us contained because feedback can sometimes be a rude awakening. As we find ourselves comparing someone else's accomplishments to our own, we must be aware of our own limiting thoughts that may attempt to impede our self-exploration. Some people will stop here feeling they cannot evolve any further and thus, succumb to self-pity and eventual misery, while others will challenge their thought processes and consider the opportunity before them. The right perspective will pay dividends.

Learn to Think

How we are taught to think determines the follow-on path we choose. If we choose correctly, we will slowly but surely become enlightened to the possibilities that present themselves to us and how they can advance our development. As we analyze those who have come before us, we are wise to do our own self-discovery. The fundamental questions of existence such as, "Who am I and what is my purpose" will create an awakening to explore if our awareness is primed with curiosity, a desire for continued evolution, and a belief that life holds something grander for us.

During this journey, we will learn of our ever-expanding capabilities and what purpose they can serve our continued expansion as human beings. Here is another tricky juncture. Some fear the feedback loop; others dive in headfirst. Those who have an open and curious mind fare best. Those who learn to believe, seek, and gear up for the evolutionary opportunity before them will grow. Those who do not grow will suffer and slowly perish into the drudgery of mediocrity. This book is not for those who wish to remain mediocre or subpar.

This is a book for those who want to learn how to become more aware of their capabilities and the inward journey they must endeavor in order to discover who they can become. It's by asking these fundamental questions that we learn of ubiquitous potentialities that can awaken us to our superpowers for advanced evolution. My suggestion: Dive in headfirst, my friends. Dive in. And as you swim around in this new reality of what is possible for you, you will then be able to see how to turn your ordinary powers into that which I call your superpowers.

Superpowers and Awareness

Superpowers by definition are powers that are superior in nature. A little vague, I suppose, but to know that something is available to you that is superior in nature is quite exciting, don't you think? Our superpowers don't just jump out at us all at once. They reveal themselves in degrees of awareness because all that is available to us is first available through the degree of our own awareness. Without awareness of a thing's existence it cannot purposefully serve us. It lay dormant until we activate it through conscious and deliberate use.

As I journeyed in life becoming more and more aware of my surroundings, the accomplishments of others, and the various life styles of the multitudes, I realized how little I truly knew of that which I was capable. I began to study the success traits of those who inspired me, those listed in each chapter that follows. What I realized is that each of these people had access to ordinary abilities, and when they combined other elements with them, something amazing usually followed; and that's when I realized that we all have access to superpowers; powers that are superior in nature.

These people were superior in nature because they used their ordinary abilities in a superior manner. I realized that superpowers are the result of the compilation of ordinary human abilities that require deliberate focus in a certain way, and when I combined a secondary element, it created a superpower that contributed to maximizing my life results.

The more I understood this concept the hungrier I became to evolve. A new shift had occurred in my mind and my perspective pivoted. Soon thereafter, I recognized the veil of darkness lifting.

The human powers that we're accustomed to, and often minimize because we don't know their true value, become superior in nature when we apply a specific focus and intention for their use. It is in this manner that we become introduced to their intended purpose: to advance our lives, the lives of others, and society as a whole. Unfortunately, we are rarely, if ever, taught to take the time to investigate how far our abilities can be stretched or leveraged, and rarely, if ever, are we taught how to combine our abilities in order to gain superior power over our lives. No, most of us were left to wander through life much like our parents did because what they were exposed to they then exposed us to. It is incumbent upon you to shift and create a new path for yourself in life and it starts with gaining a greater awareness of the superpowers you have access to.

Mind-Power

Although we mere mortals lack the commercialized superpowers of our beloved Marvel friends, we certainly do not lack the superpower inherent in our minds - we are only unaware of its potential. Many never even visit their mind nor do they ask it to reveal the answers they seek. Instead, they have a tendency to look outside of themselves for the direction and answers they so desperately need, which often leads to greater confusion and inner turmoil. Commanding our own minds and combining our ordinary abilities are techniques many are not familiar with.

Mind-power, when used in a certain way, will produce uncommon results. In fact, we have powers of the mind most cannot fathom because they lack faith in the basic principle of *possibility,* yet there is a man who was born without arms or legs who has climbed Mt. Kilimanjaro, and there is a man named Elon Musk who heads the efforts to expand space travel to Mars. Have they tapped into their superpowers? I do believe they have. So how is it that they can achieve so much yet there are millions who struggle to feel a basic sense of self-value or fulfillment? Why the drastic difference in their quality of lives?

I believe one group has discovered their superpowers and the other has not. The other lacks awareness in what *is* possible and often lacks in faith. These types of people kill the experiment before it even has a chance to prove a potential hypothesis. The difference between a man with no limbs who molds life to his will and the man who hates his life is that the first is focused on what can become reality and the second is focused on what appears to be reality. Again, it always boils down to our level of awareness and our ability to assimilate that awareness into our current lives. Awareness is an ordinary ability; assimilating its content turns it into a superpower.

Sir Roger Bannister

Another great example of someone who tapped into his superpowers is Sir Roger Bannister, a British middle distance runner, and later a renowned neuroscientist, who became the first person in record history to run a mile in under four minutes. No one in history had ever achieved such a feat. Because he did it once, others have now done it many times over. How was he able to use an ordinary ability like running and turn it into a superpower?

He started with what Napoleon Hill called a burning desire and became deliberate in his research, his use of acquired medical knowledge relating to the mechanics of running, and then devised his own athletic training program in order to become the first person to achieve his record-breaking time. He took an ordinary ability (running) and purposefully turned it into his superpower through deliberate intention by way of research and purposeful planning. He proved that once one person achieves something previously thought to be impossible; the mental block dissolves and others gain greater courage and confidence in themselves to exceed previously accepted limitations.

Can you use this same technique in your own life? You bet you can! The primary requirement is to have an intention to do something great with your ordinary abilities and then become relentless in your focus and execution. Did you catch that? Reread it again.

Indomitable Spirit

Using your superpowers starts by acknowledging that it is actually possible to accomplish an extraordinary result using an ordinary ability in a certain way. The only limits before you are the ones you self-impose or accept. Does it require an indomitable spirit? You damn right it does. This isn't the land of fairytales and ladybugs. History has proven that what was once thought of as impossible was only impossible until someone made it possible. That requires a part of you to come alive that you may not even know lives within you. The first step is always a shift in perspective, which comes from having faith in your emerging awareness. Take for instance the word "impossible". One person will read it as "impossible", another will read it as "*I'm possible*". Perspective is everything. Perspective is born of awareness. Awareness is born of continual exposure.

One of the great historical accounts of what is possible when using one's superpowers is that of the Wright brothers: Wilbur and Orville were American inventors and pioneers of aviation. According to the History Channel, they achieved the first sustained and controlled self-propelled airplane flight in 1903, and by 1909, the U.S. Signal Corps purchased a specially constructed plane that would be the beginning of a new era for civilization.

Can you image what people must've thought of them prior to successfully achieving flight? They were probably thought to be crazy. Who in the world, especially during the late 1800s and early 1900s, would've thought these two men were sane. Bicycles had only just become the new craze. Bicycles! And here they were trying to invent something to fly in the air on its own. What inspired these two young men to be so outrageous in their expectations? They turned their ordinary powers of vision, fascination, passion, and curiosity into their superpowers by fueling them with focus, purpose, imagination, emotion, and the power of an indomitable spirit toward success through relentless dedication. Now it's yours turn. Will you meet the challenge?

More Amazing Examples

Here are a few more ordinary people who exemplify the indomitable spirit by having used their ordinary powers in a manner earning them the right to lay claim to their superpowers. You, too, can join the ranks of such amazing people if you dare.

1. Jessica Cox is the world's first armless pilot and black belt in Taekwondo.
2. Kris Dim is a paralyzed pro bodybuilder.
3. Nathan Sawaya quit his job as a lawyer and became a LEGO artist.
4. Andrei Rosu wanted to get in shape and set a good example for his son so he began working out. He became the first person to complete 7 marathons and 7 ultra-marathons on 7 different continents. He also became the first man to play drums at the North Pole.

5. Maura Ward was diagnosed with Parkinson's at age sixty-four. For her sixty-fifth birthday, she skydived for the first time and raised a bunch of money for a Parkinson's charity.

6. Anjan Manikumar's restaurant in downtown Toronto is completely staffed by deaf waiters and waitresses.

7. Candy Lightener founded Mothers Against Drunk Driving (MADD) in her home on March 7, 1980 after her 13-year-old daughter was killed by a repeat DWI offender. Before MADD, there were little to no legal consequences for driving while intoxicated. Her organization transformed American attitudes about drunk driving and successfully fought for stricter laws across the country.

8. Lilly Ledbetter sued Good Year for paying her less over the decades than her male coworkers. After reaching the Supreme Court and being denied a ruling in her favor, Justice Ruth Bader Ginsberg wrote a stirring dissent, which led to Congress subsequently passing the Lilly Ledbetter Fair Pay Act in 2009,

changing federal law to better protect women in the workplace.

Each one of these exemplars was faced with a choice about the quality of life they wanted to create for themselves. Most of them faced impediments that could've asphyxiated their hope but instead, they found the courage to believe in something greater than their doubts, and because of that belief, they produced extraordinary results. That's how you transform ordinary power into superpower.

What's required?

An indomitable belief in miracles.

These people are just like you and me, but something inspired them to have extreme focus and dedication. Maybe they knew if they didn't, their soul would slowly die. They used what threatened their livelihood and turned it into their superpower. What I want you to know is that it's possible for you, too. When you intentionally set out to do something specific and you add elements of laser focus, intentionality, desire, and all the other forces necessary in a concerted manner, you gain superior power. This is the path of turning your ordinary powers into superpowers. Imagine what that can mean for you. Imagine what you can accomplish. Imagine how you can change the world. Imagine how you can catapult your life while also advancing society. That's the shit I'm talking about. That's living a super powered life!

You Are Not Ordinary

As you continue to read on, consider that which you may not have ever considered before: that you, ordinary you, are actually in possession of superpowers. All you need to do is *decide* you no longer want to be ordinary, and then begin. Inch by inch it becomes a cinch. From this day forward, you can never live an average or below average life again because you now know that you have power within you that awaits unleashing. It begs to be unleashed. It's been faintly tugging at your heart. Have you not felt it? Of course you have. It's the voice being squelched by your daily frustrations. Why have you not acknowledged it? Has no one taught you? Have your limiting beliefs gotten in the way? Has lack of knowledge stifled your growth? Well, no longer. You have now been awakened.

You must begin to affirm the incredible phenomenon that is you. Your potential is unfathomable for no one knows what brews deep within you. Limitations are all theory until someone proves them otherwise. YOU are that someone.

Has anyone ever told you that you can actually change the world? YES, YOU! You can actually change the world. And if you don't want to change the world, you can at least change your world. Do you believe it? You need to because it's true!

2

The Superpower
Inherent in Your Awareness

"The key to growth is the introduction of higher dimensions of consciousness into our awareness."

~ Lao Tzu

No behavior, action, or thought can be identified as healthy or unhealthy until an awareness of the meaning of such terms is gained.

I find it fascinating in my line of work as a mental health therapist, and in retrospect of my own evolution, how it's possible that people can be at a different level of awareness of the same exact social construct. Take something as common as finances, for instance. One person uses their credit card frivolously and gets into debt, while a different person understands the consequences of irresponsible spending, and thus is wise in their financial discipline. What's the primary difference between the two people? Their awareness level.

According to Merriam-Webster dictionary, awareness is defined as the knowledge and understanding that something is happening or exists. In essence, it's the ability of your mind to monitor and analyze your inner being and external circumstances, while taking into account the likely rewards and consequences of your actions. Awareness is your capacity to recognize a construct, which is generated by the neural connections in your brain. The more environmental and intellectual exposure you have to knowledge and wisdom, the more aware you will become of the elements, rewards, and consequences of situations and the possibilities that are available to you. For example, there are some people who dream of a better life. Maybe they were exposed to the possibility of having a better life through their exposure to the life styles of others, or by reading books, magazines, or viewings through the media.

Conversely, there are others who lack all awareness of the possibility of creating a better life for themselves because they've never been exposed to such a philosophy. It doesn't currently exist in their belief system because it doesn't exist in their worldview. Does that sound improbable in a world where rags to riches stories are plentiful? It did to me for many years before I gained wisdom through self-education, ultimately realizing that just because something is in plain sight does not mean that everyone has the same awareness level of its existence. Understanding this semantic changed my life and my ability to help others increase their own awareness.

Emotional Connection for a New Paradigm

Many years ago while suffering my own inner turmoil due to a general lack of awareness, it was brought to my attention that there are people who travel to warm destinations during the winter months to avoid cold weather. This resonated with me on an emotional level because I abhor cold weather. Since I had an interest in the topic of discussion, I inherently had an intense emotional connection to the idea. So, since I abhor winters, my consciousness allowed the possibility that I, too, could travel to a warmer climate to escape the cold. I found that once I became open to the possibility of something being true for me, my brain became alert to ways of making it happen.

One winter while working on my PhD, I remembered someone had previously mentioned they rented a condo on an island through a website. I knew the time away would enhance my focus, so that winter I rented a condo in Puerto Rico for three months, and the very next year, I rented another condo in St. Thomas. Why was I able to incorporate this practice into my lifestyle, while others cannot? Because I accepted the idea as a viable possibility. My awareness level expanded to this new belief and then I took action. Many people discount new ideas because they immediately think of all the reasons they feel it's impossible for them. So since they focus on the impossibility of it being doable, they leave no room for strategizing its implementation.

There are some people who are awestruck that I'm able to take winters off or that my career takes me to tropical islands. They think it's not possible for them, but that's just not true. It could be possible if they had an open mind. The truth is we can do anything we want to do; we just need to have the mindset of making it possible in order to have all universal sources working in our favor, both those that we directly control and those that we do not. Creative solutions only flow when we are open-minded to potentialities. Too many people kill great ideas in their infancy by sheer disbelief and cynicism. Remember, your reality is first created in your mind through greater awareness, which then becomes a new belief, and with purposeful focus, manifestation can occur.

Ask How to Find Solutions

I learned years ago to ask "how" I can make something happen, instead of justifying why it's not possible. Your brain will assist and obey you in either scenario, so it behooves you to teach it to find opportunities and solutions. This is how you begin to deliberately create your life.

Another common example is our ability to attend college. There are some youth who have never heard of the term college and therefore are unaware of not only what it is but why it might be important for their future. How can that be when throngs of young people leave high school every year to attend college? The answer in this example is not very different from the previous example of credit card use. It's their lack of exposure to specific information on a consistent basis for internalization, which determines why some people are "in the know" and others are oblivious.

When information is repetitively presented to people and they are encouraged to assimilate the content with an emotional connection then it increases awareness by way of the visceral experience one has when receiving the information into their consciousness. Again, just because something is in plain sight does not mean everyone is aware of it. Just because someone might hear about college does not mean they understand the concept or its purpose. It could literally go in one ear and out the other because it has not been personalized or imbedded into their consciousness. The same is true for any other concept that the masses are thought to have common knowledge of.

(Side note: I advise you to get extended wise counsel before deciding to attend college to ensure you pick a major that will indeed lead you to becoming employed after graduation. There are many people who spend tens of thousands of dollars on college degrees and then cannot get a job, or if they do, it may not pay enough to live a financially stable or abundant life. Research the concept of "degree mills" and also consider how you can create at least 3 sources of income from your major. If not, I would strongly recommend you reconsidering that major because student loan debt will stop you from being able to purchase a home. At the same time, higher education is vital to your development. It doesn't have to come in the form of a 4 year degree or a PhD. Conduct thorough research before you decide.)

How Do We Learn?

Our primary means for learning is through exposure. If we are not exposed to more intelligent ways of living, we can literally live our entire lives without being none-the-wiser. This is why reading personal growth and development books are so critically important to increasing your level of awareness. Can you believe someone can have 15 kids and never consider what it takes to be a good parent? It's mind-boggling but it's happening all around us. Lack of awareness is the fundamental culprit.

Obviously, everyone grows up differently due to individual genetics, socioeconomic status, culture, community influences, home rearing, quality of education, and exposure to the media, etc. There arc countless examples of things some people are aware of and consider common sense, while others are clueless to the facts. Here's a short list of what some have a healthy awareness of that others unfortunately do not:

1. Daily habits create your life
2. Qualities of a healthy mate
3. Importance of a dedicated work ethic
4. Intelligent behaviors to stay out of legal trouble

5. Reading to your children enhances their futures
6. The importance of a good night's sleep
7. Following your passion or calling in life instead of working a meaningless and unfulfilling job
8. The importance of self-care, self-control, self-respect, and good hygiene.
9. Yelling is unhealthy for everyone

How is it that some of these are so obvious to some people while other people lack awareness? Aren't these basic principles universal? Yes, they are, but there are so many different cultures, environmental influences, parenting styles, ideals, traditions, education levels, access to better employment opportunities, etc. that preclude common sense from being common. This is why it's incumbent upon us all to continue challenging our beliefs and advancing our self-education.

Parents need to realize they probably know very little about actually being a good parent because there's no basis for us to believe we know how to actually parent children correctly. Did any of us take a class given by an expert? No, most of us did not. We're all winging it and winging parenting skills is the stupidest thing people can do, and yet, we all do it. We spend 12-23 years, and even more in classroom settings (primary, secondary, and collegiate years) learning academic material that we rarely use later in life, and yet, the one thing everyone needs to learn, good parenting skills to raise a productive member of society, is never taught to us in a formal setting. It's asinine if you really think about it.

People need to be taught through deliberate exposure to information in order to increase their awareness. The lack of teaching and the lack of exposure both lead to ignorance. Even the skill of "paying attention" needs to be specifically taught because humans are programed to find the path of least resistance. Many times children don't want to be where they are, such as in school, so they become great at daydreaming and checking out of life, which reduces their ability to increase their awareness level. If our brains are not stimulated properly, we get bored very quickly. It's through paying attention in life that we increase our awareness, so we need to learn how to be present.

The Importance of Neural Connections

As the conscious mind is exposed to information from the environment (parents, peer groups, school, social media, etc.), the information will either be accepted or rejected. If accepted, the subconscious mind will begin to program itself through the creation of neural connections. The more repetitive the information, the stronger the subconscious programming. It's important that we understand we're constantly being exposed to information and we have the power to reject it if it's not going to wield us healthy results, but this requires an awareness, which comes from being taught by someone. If we don't reject unhealthy information, behaviors, emotions, or experiences immediately, our brains will simulate the information and later require a reprogramming to change those neural connections. As the saying goes, it's easier to do things right in the beginning than to try to correct it later.

Our brains are trained how to think by every incoming stimuli from infancy until death. The bad news is the more unhealthy our environment when we are younger, the harder it is to reprogram our brain in adulthood due to the established neural connections, and how they affect our nervous system. The good news is that we know the brain can be retrained due to the current research on neuroplasticity. To become aware of anything new requires our consciousness to be introduced to new information over a period of time in order for the information to be assimilated. This is how we can deliberately increase our own awareness level. Again, this is why reading personal growth and development books is vitally important, as is being exposed to several mentors (online and in person), having the mindset to seek people out who are performing at higher levels in life than you are, and to maintain a growth perspective throughout one's life as opposed to a perspective of complacency, self-righteousness, or limiting beliefs.

Expand Your Awareness

Continually seeking to expand your awareness level allows you to gain a deeper understanding of yourself, those around you, and your physical environment through objective analysis. It helps you gain greater control over your thoughts and emotions enabling you to cultivate a healthy lifestyle based on healthier decision-making. Your awareness level becomes your superpower when you become aware of its purpose for your life. Most people never consider their awareness level; it's just not a very common topic of discussion and so they miss the opportunity to use it as a superpower. By simply becoming aware that there is such a thing as "your awareness level", and by purposefully increasing it, you automatically increase the potential for your quality of life (and life expectancy), thus, awakening your dormant powers.

Now that you have awakened to its potential for improving your life, imagine what you can achieve once you deliberately and continually empower your awareness through purposeful use of it. You can begin to shift from being primarily motivated by emotion and instinct to greater use of your logic and reasoning faculties. You can now take control of your life, maybe for the very first time ever! You will begin to awaken to the elements around you and you'll see your life in a way you never have before. You can stop being deceived, manipulated, abused, controlled, and stunted in your growth, whether by your own limiting thoughts, emotions, and environment or by other people's, and instead begin asking yourself some very good questions like:

- What in the hell is really going on in my life?
- Who am I?
- Am I happy?
- What am I doing with my time and focus every day?
- How have I allowed others to control my life?
- Why am I allowing someone else to control my life?
- Have I been mistreating people?
- Am I lazy, controlling, rude or narcissistic, and if so, why?
- Am I reliving my past?
- Am I a prisoner in my own mind?

- How long have I been complaining about the same problems and not doing anything to fix them?
- Why do I drink and smoke so much?
- Why have I allowed myself to become so physically, emotionally, mentally, financially, and psychologically unhealthy?
- What am I truly afraid of?
- How did I get stuck?
- What 1 thing can I do to begin getting unstuck?
- What do I need?
- Who do I need to forgive?
- How can I give myself permission to forgive myself and stop wasting my life?
- What can I change today?

And you start awakening to the new philosophy of:
- I control my life, no one else does.
- I am powerful beyond measure.
- I am a good person.
- If I can dream it, I can achieve it because I believe in limitless potential.

- The only limitations on my life are the ones I accept.

- My mind use to limit me, but not anymore.

- I can figure out how to fix my life and I can get help to fix it to ensure quicker results.

- I can invest in a life coach to learn shortcuts because investing in myself is the best investment I will ever make.

- Abuse in any form is unhealthy and I will not tolerate it.

- I can stop being motivated by momentary impulses and instead objectively assess situations.

- Contributing to the greater good of society now motivates me.

- I can observe what is going on inside of me and be guided by what's in my best interest.

- I can stop arguing and screaming at people because that's not the kind of person I want to be.

- I need to spend more quality time with my children reading and playing with them.

- I want to live a healthier life so I will be more mindful of what I put in my body.
- I absolutely can Design my own Destiny with Dr. Cruz!
- No weapon formed against me shall prosper!

It was Tony Robbins who kindly reminded us that, *"The quality of one's life is directly related to the quality of questions one asks oneself",* and by Jim Rohn who stated, *"Your personal philosophy is the greatest determining factor of how your life will turn out."* By asking better questions and creating a new life philosophy you will awaken your awareness to your superpowers! My hope is that this chapter has begun this process for you and you now supersede all previous oblivion. Believe that you are now able to take flight into a limitless life of your own divine creation because you have been set free! Say that and say it often. "I can now take flight into a limitless life of my own divine creation because I have been set free!

3

The Superpower of Clarity

"There are few things more powerful than a life lived with passionate clarity." ~ Erwin McManus

Listen up! This is one of the most important superpowers available to you, so please pay very close attention.

The message is very clear: *Gain Clarity!*

There's nothing quite as important to execution as first gaining clarity. Clarity is the state of being crystal clear and free of any ambiguity for that which you desire to attain. It is best thing going next to execution. Clarity and execution are real superpowers. Clarity is achieved when you can see exactly what you want to achieve in your mind's eye. Without it, you'll either delay or fail in achieving that which you set out for. You can save years of wasted man-hours when you are crystal clear about your goals and the associated steps to obtain your goal. Conversely: neglect gaining clarity and you'll wander lost.

If you want to achieve a specific goal, you must be crystal-clear about where exactly the bull's-eye that you want to hit is. What does it looks like? If you're not crystal clear on those two things nothing else will matter. When you take a road trip you must know the exact address to put in your GPS or else you won't arrive at your exact location. The same is true for goals. Has someone ever given you vague instructions only to later tell you that what you provided is not what they asked for? Did they lack clarity in the directions they gave you? Probably. Clarity is vital for success. Without it, you're wasting your time.

Don't Be the Average Person

The average person does not usually have crystal clear clarity about anything. They might feel something, want something, or have an idea for something but if you ask them what their first seven steps to achieving it is, you may very well be met with a blank face. When you lack clarity you lack specificity. So ask yourself, "What is my bull's-eye"? Do you want to earn 7 figures as a real estate agent? Do you want to travel to Spain and Greece next summer for three weeks in July? Do you want to weigh 140 pounds? Do you want to dress more professionally in business suits to increase your self-esteem and project a new image? Do you want to create a nonprofit and financially sponsor 1,000 families next Thanksgiving? Do you want to author a New York Times #1 best seller? Do you want to pay off your home in 3 years? Do you want to own a business selling products that enhance the health of your customers? Do you want to be a great stay-at-home mom? What do you want? You must know this before you can decide on the strategy to achieve it.

"What do you want" is the most important question you can ask yourself. Ponder it in great detail. Your brain is like a heat seeking missile and if you give it coordinates, it will do everything in its power to ensure the target is hit. It works 24 hours a day, 7 days a week for you but it does not consciously think on its own. You must learn to think in order to gain crystal-clear clarity.

Step 1:

At least 1-3x a week go to a quiet place and meditate. Bring a pen and paper with you, or even better, turn your phone's voice recorder on so when you receive revelation you don't interrupt the flow of incoming information by opening your eyes to write. Instead, you can verbally describe your revelations as they show up in your mind's eye. I cannot impress upon you enough how important it is to write or otherwise record your God inspired thoughts and feelings. This is Divine intervention; Divine communication. It usually happens very quickly and is either a very soft voice or idea. If it comes across as a vision, many times it's a very quick glimpse. PAY ATTENTION! Be present and alert to what may show up for you. Stay ready so you don't have to get ready. It might seem like an insignificant feeling but it very well could be the life changing idea you've been waiting on. Honor it by acknowledging and recording it.

Step 2

Describe your vision as if you are trying to explain it to a kindergartner and a CEO at the same time. Be clear on the overall picture of the goal you want to achieve. Example: I want to weigh 140 pounds by July 30th. That is a targeted goal. Then write out the steps you need to take to achieve it. You would be surprised how many people say they know this but don't do it. Humans like to overestimate their effectiveness instead of going back to basics. So if by weighing 140 pounds by July 30th is the exact address you want to put in your proverbial GPS, what are the step-by-step instructions the GPS would provide for you in return that even a kindergarten and a CEO could follow? For example:

- Monday, Wednesday, and Friday 60 minutes of cardio: Two minutes of jumping jacks, 20 minutes running, 20 minutes row machine, 18 minutes on elliptical machine.

- Saturday: Meditate 20 minutes and 45 minutes of yoga.
- Sunday: 3 mile walk with my significant other and dog.
- Diet: only drink water. Only eat wild salmon, chicken, sushi, broccoli, Cheerios with bananas and almond milk.
- Snacks: cucumbers and 7 almonds a day.
- Dessert: 5 vanilla wafers.
- Seven days a week: 5 minutes of visualizing myself at 140 pounds before getting out of bed. Talk to my 140 pound self in the mirror and congratulate her everyday on her progress. That's what crystal clear clarity looks like. It's very precise.

Inviting Divine Intervention

Writing out your vision, your plan, and your strategy every day will also advance you in a way others won't benefit because they lack the discipline to do the work. This is called journaling and most people skip this step. They say it's too much work or they already know what they need to do. "I got this", many will say but what they neglect to remember is that God is in the details. As you take the time to write and rewrite your goals and strategies every day, divine intervention is invited to show up. If you don't sit down and do the work you're not giving divine intervention an opportunity to show up and interject its influence. You see, most people think it's them who is achieving the goal but that's only partially true. People of excellence aren't excellent at birth. They grow and develop into excellent people first based on a decision to go in that direction and then by doing the work but their work is different than that of the average person. That's why they're different. Their clarity is defined so their strategies are engineered uniquely.

So do yourself a favor and discipline yourself to write out your vision, plans, and strategies every day and if you're really serious about achieving your goals, write them out two times a day. Give yourself 10 minutes every morning and evening to do this because it will wield you greater clarity on how to achieve your goals. There's also a neurological effect that works for you. Consider that you are continuously reminding and recalibrating your own GPS system. Your subconscious mind is your GPS. Program it! You must be the cheetah and not the gazelle when it comes to creating clarity for your life. Attack it with authority. Remember time waits for no one so get to work.

30,000 Days

There are several ways to enhance your clarity and it is incumbent upon you to make these exercises a priority in your life as soon as possible not just for your benefit but for the benefit of your children and grandchildren. Are they important to you? The more important they are to you the more likely gaining clarity will be a priority for you. One of the best gifts you can give them is explaining the importance of them gaining their own individual clarity in life. You can give them a copy of this book since it already explains it for them. In fact, a better gift would be a copy of this book with a handwritten letter from you explaining that we all have about 30,000 days to get everything we want done in our lives, so the sooner we're clear on the direction we need to move in life the sooner we will achieve it. Clarity helps us not to get lost in life. *Clarity is a superpower because most people overlook it.*

Exercise:

1. Journal with the intention to gain clarity. Journaling is a great exercise all the way around. I can't imagine anyone finding a negative thing to say about journaling. When you journal with a specific purpose in mind, especially that of mining information to gain specific direction, you turn an average ability into a superpower. Intentionality is the magic potion. Let's say you're not sure what career field you want to endeavor. You can begin by journaling your thoughts and ideas on the top five careers that interest you. Do your research on each career field and identify things such as qualifications needed, expected salary, options for growth, and the pulse of that particular job market. Is there a state licensure required? What motivates your interest in this field? Is it strong enough to

sustain a 10-20 year career that feeds your passion? Whose lives will you enhance by participating in this field of work?

I recommend writing this personal exercise out several times over a period of three months to solidify your knowing. It's important to gain crystal clear clarity on the work that will make you feel significant in the world and emotionally fulfilled. When you go back to reread your journal entries, greater clarity will come over you as to whether or not it's in alignment with your calling. Journaling has a magic about it that facilitates clarity.

4

The Superpower of Identifying Your Life's Purpose

"The purpose of human life is to serve, and to show compassion and the will to help others."
~ Albert Schweitzer

Let's just get right to the point of life!

The real meaning of life does not start until we find our purpose. Anything we do prior to finding our purpose is an attempt to construct our lives without realizing that as smart as we think we are, we usually get this part wrong. The topic of finding our purpose often confuses people because they feel they have to find the "one" thing in life that they were called to do. In this way, it's framed as finding a needle in haystack. My aim is to introduce you to a new approach.

When I first started considering what my life's purpose was I initially thought it was to be a mental health therapist but the more I endeavored, the more I learned it was not. I realized that being a mental health therapist was just one way I could *express* my purpose. Then I thought maybe it was to be a life coach, a public speaker, an advocate for literacy, and a provider of safe housing for foster care alumni, but again, the more I endeavored the more I realized these also were just avenues through which I could *express* my purpose. My framework for understanding my life's purpose was wrong. The question wasn't so much what was I supposed to be doing with my life; the question was who was I born to become? Do you know who you were born to become? Most people do not.

Who Are You At Your Core?

When I realized that at my core I am a helper for the people's healing, my confusion started to dissipate. It became clearer to me that my purpose was to help people mentally and emotionally heal. This was my authentic purpose. How I allowed that to manifest was within my control. So, instead of conceptualizing my identity from societal credentials, I borrowed my creator's eyes. Who had he created me to become? The answer that was revealed to me was that I am a healer of the mind because that's where all suffering originates.

To figure out who you are you must peel back the layers of who you have become because who you've become is not necessarily who you authentically are, or even who you were meant to become. Who you have become represents the roles you've taken on in life or the roles projected upon you by others such as your parents, other family members, friends, teachers, etc., so you must peel back those layers. Who are you underneath the family role you have taken on as a mother, father, daughter, or son? Who are you under your social standings, educational credentials, military rank, bank account balance, and the color of your skin? Who are you in a metaphysical sense? What do you know about yourself on a molecular level? What do you feel strongly about? What really matters to you? What do you stand for? What would you fight for?

I have found that our purpose is usually correlated to our natural talents and interests to which we are drawn toward. So let's start there. What are your natural talents and interests? What are you being drawn toward? Now dig deeper. What calls you from within your spirit? You don't need to feel you're necessarily good at the particular thing you're being called toward because you can and will get better at it once you begin purposefully engaging in it, so relax any critical judgments that may surface. Just identify what calls you from within your spirit. For instance, I always wanted to help people probably because I needed help myself and no one was sufficiently qualified to help me. I may not have been very good at appropriately helping people early on but I got better at it the more I understood the psychology of people. I studied my craft and became a life coach, a licensed mental health clinician, and a hypnotherapist. I'm always growing my skills in ways that will better help others and because I do, I never feel depressed or bored. I realize I have **unquantifiable** worth. *If you apply yourself toward your calling and link it to helping others advance in life, you, too, will realize you have unquantifiable worth, as well!*

Your Life's Purpose

You may have a latent calling in your spirit that has been overshadowed by life demands. When you were younger, did you feel you were called to do something specific like writing? I was, but I later learned that writing wasn't my actual calling. It was just an avenue of expression for what was in my spirit. It was one way in which I could help more people. But that is my personal story. If you are called to write, your life's purpose may be to become a prolific writer.

Everyone's purpose in life is different. It is our own unique footprint as we walk through life. No one can tell you what your life purpose is but those closest to you may be able to give you some insight about what they sense you're good at, which may be hidden from your own awareness. When identified and focused upon properly, your life's purpose can create for you an ever lasting legacy that will positively affect the lives of people who have not even been born yet. This is some exciting stuff, I assure you.

When you think of your purpose it will always be associated with helping or advancing the lives of others in some way, shape, or form. Our life's purpose is never solely for our own selfish pleasure. So we must keep in mind that our life's purpose is not really about us, per se. We are only the vehicles. There is someone in society that will gain the benefit of your natural talents and abilities when channeled through your life's purpose. If you are unaware of your life's purpose, don't fret. Life is about self-discovery so rest-assure that in time you will discover your purpose if you intend to do so. Be interested in it and it will reveal itself to you.

Over time, if you find that you cannot figure out your purpose, you can just pick a purpose based on your interests because again, in time you will realize what is and is not in alignment with your spirit. Just stay alert and you will begin to be led. When I was younger, I thought I wanted to be a lawyer. Like many foster children, I was exposed to quite a few lawyers because we are constantly in and out of family court, so maybe they intrigued me. Personally, I think I would've been a great lawyer, but I've since learned that there's a difference between our passion and our purpose. I had a fondness for helping people, so being a lawyer was a viable option for me based on my lack of exposure to other viable options. Had I taken that path for sake of not knowing a better path to take, it would have eventually either satisfied my purpose in life or it would have led me to a more aligned expression of my purpose.

The point is that where we start off in life does not have to determine where we end. With an awakened mind, we will constantly recalibrate our path as we design our destiny. So had I just chosen to be a lawyer for lack of greater clarity, I would have eventually realized that that was or was not the best path for me to pursue. It would **not** have been a waste of my time because all life experience contributes to our growth when growth is what we're focused on. Obviously though, we want to narrow-in on and identify the best path to pursue our life's purpose as soon as possible in order to live congruently and reduce any mental, physical, or spiritual dissonance.

In retrospect, I can see that maybe I thought I could "help" people by working as a lawyer. There is, after all, more than one way to skin a cat, right? Yes, there is but we need to keep in mind the value of time. We are not going to live forever so we want to allocate our time wisely. In your own life, make sure you consult your spirit. As long as you feel you're headed in the right direction, you are living congruently in that moment. The path of life is not linear. Ultimately, all life experience has purpose.

The Gifts of Finding Your Purpose

Once you figure out what your unique purpose is, you immediately enhance your degree of inner peace, happiness, sense of significance, confidence, identity, etc., and reduce your stress, aloofness, and sense of worthlessness. If you allow your purpose to be your life's guide, everything that follows will improve your life. You can then branch out and decide how much money you want to make, where you want to live, and what population of people you want to contribute to. You will also be able to reduce any negative thoughts that race through your mind, any sadness, physical illness, boredom, or misery, etc. because by following the path of your life's purpose you inherently increase the quality of your life.

You will feel excited about waking up in the morning and living, instead of just enduring and existing. You will feel fulfilled as you contribute to society. You will be able to then learn multiple ways to generate income from your work, which increases your ability to continue to help others in need. The more you are aligned with your purpose the more energy you'll have to expand your business. Yes, you will get tired like everyone else but you'll wake up refreshed and be ready to go again for another fruitful day. Your daily stamina will be augmented by internal motivation. After all, you'll be living in alignment with your life's purpose, which is the main reason you were born. The goal is to get all cylinders firing in the same direction to propel and sustain you. There is where your superpower lives.

Your purpose starts out as a beacon, creates a path for you to follow, evolves into a mission, and can make you independently wealthy in finances, health, love, and happiness. You will be able to multiply your efforts more easily because you will likely develop an indomitable spirit toward the success you inevitably will begin pursuing. Scientific research tells us that individuals with a sense of purpose are happier and have a larger net worth than those whose lives lack meaning. Purpose equates to your life having real meaning!

Researchers correlate people who feel their life has meaning with being more goal-oriented. Now keep in mind, you can be goal-oriented toward something that is not your life's purpose, but why would you want to be that person? You don't! Take for instance the founder of Victoria's

Secret, Roy Raymond. Victoria's Secret, now a billion dollar company, was initially founded in 1977 and later sold to a sportswear mogul named Leslie Wexner due to Raymond's financial struggles. Combined with other life struggles to include the failures of at least two other businesses, Raymond ended his life by jumping off San Francisco's Golden Gate Bridge. I can only assume that he lost focus of his life's purpose and fell victim to the pressures of extreme debt, a sense of failure, and defeat, all which overtook him. When we stay focused on our life's purpose we can avoid such tragedy and instead live a long, meaningful life.

5

The Superpower of Giving Yourself Permission

"Dream and give yourself permission to envision a you
that you choose to be."
~ Joy Page

I've heard it said that there are people who do not think they deserve happiness, success, or even love. I often wonder why someone would feel that they don't deserve these things. Well, there are many reasons I suppose, namely a lack of self-esteem, self-love, being guilt ridden, and not knowing who they are in Christ, etc. Some people are just plain scared and need to give themselves permission to think highly enough of themselves to release the chains that bind them. What are these chains that bind people? Where do they come from? And who locks us up in them in the first place?

Identifying the Chains

These chains can be mental or physical and to make it even more of a curious enigma, these chains can be real or figments of our perception. How can that be? Well, these chains that bind us and hinder our growth are mostly in our mind. They are generated from perspective and become our belief systems. Beliefs such as:

- That's not possible for people like me
- No one loves me
- I'm not smart enough
- I don't know how, etc.

The fundamental point is that limiting beliefs limit one's ability to walk in faith, think appropriately, and create strategies to design one's own destiny. Often times, these limits exist because the conversation of giving ourselves permission has never been had, thus, permission has never been granted. Permission for what, you ask. Permission to be great, permission to love ourselves, permission to put ourselves first without feeling guilty, and permission to believe in ourselves. These are all topics of conversation that must be had to increase our personal power and free ourselves to excel.

Have the Conversation

This is point #1. If we've never had the conversation we probably have never objectively considered if the option of achieving what it is we're disbelieving for ourselves is even possible. We must learn to dream, believe, and find like-minded people to have this conversation with. Has anyone ever talked to you about designing your own destiny? For countless people the answer is no. So how can we achieve something we've never discussed with another person or even ourselves? We can't.

If we've never had a conversation about it we probably are unaware of the possibilities available to us, and if we don't consider the possibilities we can't move closer to accomplishing that which is in our best interest. So have a conversation with someone about what it means to give yourself permission to be free from limitations and what you can then believe possible for yourself. This will allow the universe to begin to work in your favor because your mind will begin to awaken, which is a prerequisite to receiving your blessings.

Give yourself permission

Give yourself permission to believe it's possible! Whatever you want to do or achieve, believe that you can achieve it so your heart will be rooted in it. Get out of your limiting mind and get into your greatness! Give yourself permission to deserve it. You must acknowledge that you deserve the absolute best in life. If you don't give yourself permission to believe that, you can't receive the miracle. You'll find yourself getting stuck, unable to move into position. It's solely up to you to give yourself permission to do and achieve whatever it is you want. You can't wait, need, or depend on anyone else. Yes, it's very helpful and ideal to have a support system but the reality for many of us is that we don't always have one. What are we then to do? Build one!

Sometimes your only support system is you and God's Word and that has to be enough until your tribe shows up. It's not always easy and it can be a very lonely road, but we must know that we have the power to give ourselves permission to create our own support system. There will be times when our support system might include one or two people and other times we might have several people we can depend on for encouragement. There really isn't any golden rule and it's quite fluid at times. If you feel you do not have anyone who can support and encourage you to achieve your dreams it becomes your responsibility to find someone and cultivate that relationship. Ultimately, we must take personal responsibility for our needs, realize it's a process, and know that we are all works in progress. As long as your mindset is one of growth and expansion, rest assured you will find like-minded people on the way up, but until then, get comfortable being uncomfortable. It's only for a moment.

It's your life

It's your life and you only have one. You will either spend it preoccupied by self-doubt, negative self-talk, and a limited understanding of what's possible for you, or you will wake up and realize that time waits for no one. Whose responsibility is it to create your life? Whose responsibility is it to take charge of your destiny? It's yours. You. Just you. It's no one else's responsibility. This is your superpower. Own it!

Time will not wait for you to figure this stuff out. You must realize right now how finite life truly is and then get your ass in motion. It is time to wake up and realize that this is your life. THIS is your life! This is your life and you must learn to design your destiny first by acknowledging you deserve to have the life you want. Give yourself permission to be happy and then do the work.

The reality is that none of this will matter until you give yourself permission to deserve, explore, create, and execute. By virtue of being born, you deserve the absolute best in life as long as you are willing to work for it. People who do not work for their greatness do not deserve to be great. Are you willing to work for your greatness? If so, give yourself permission right now to deserve it. Give yourself permission to explore life's opportunities. They are here for you to take advantage of, but again, you must be willing to do the mental and physical work. Give yourself permission to step out on faith and execute. To execute means to take action and lots of it. Create a plan and take massive action everyday until your dream becomes a reality for you. Have faith in yourself. Have faith in your vision. Have faith in your inner voice. Step out on faith and know this is a superpower because it precedes belief.

6

The Superpower of Solving Problems

"Do not focus on money, instead focus on a problem that needs to be solved for the world. Money will follow you as a bi-product."

~ Manoj Arora

Have you ever noticed that most people spend the majority of their lives focused on themselves: what they want, don't want, have, don't have, etc. It's no wonder why addiction to substances and stress related health challenges are leading problems in America. By nature, people are very self-focused. By focusing on ourselves we suffer from negative emotional frames of reference. Why is that? Because humans are prone to self-reflect on the negative quicker than they do the positive. People can point out 10 wrong things someone has done or that they have done themselves before ever speaking on 10 right things.

Imagine, if you will, the possibilities if we would just shift our focus from the undeniable misery associated with self-focus and instead focus on what we could do for other people. This is where the good life is! This is how we receive all the good stuff we think focusing on ourselves will provide but never does. Caring for others increases our sense of well-being, our self-esteem, our understanding of what this life truly is about, and extends the years of our life, according to several scientific research studies. This is where we gain a sense of purpose. By helping to solve other people's problems we become better people. This is the magical formula for the good life, hidden in plain sight, and invisible to so many.

Science shows us that when we're invested in the benefits others will receive from our contribution, we bring value to our identities and enhance the quality of our life. Why? Because to have a good quality of life you must feel your life has meaning, and our lives never have real meaning when our focus is solely on our selfish natures.

Focus on Helping Others

This is also the core philosophy for business. Every business in existence either provides a service or a product to solve a need or desire for someone else, never for the businesses own sake. We just aren't that important: not as self-focused individuals or as businesses. There's plenty of room here to insert: GET OVER YOURSELF. The real value you possess is the value you can provide to another human being to help improve his or her life.

Understand that your skill set is your ordinary power and you turn it into a superpower by figuring out how to leverage that skill set to help others. Thereafter, you set in motion a positive chain reaction for a return on your quality of life. In this way, you increase not only your own self-esteem and sense of fulfillment but you also become a valuable member of society, while leaving a legacy for your family, all the while touching the hearts of countless people in the process. This is what makes for a good life.

It helps to remember that we only get to occupy earth for a finite amount of time and our job is not to mindlessly take up space using up all its resources unapologetically. It is, in fact, our moral obligation to contribute to society in a positive manner. This, unfortunately, is a memo everyone hasn't received yet. I, too, only received my memo when I was in my late 30s.

Contributing to society doesn't necessarily require a life saving invention. If you can make someone's life better or easier by using your God-given talents and abilities, you instantaneously create a win/win for everyone involved. And not only that, but your efforts subsequently improve the lives of secondary and tertiary beneficiaries. It's quite possible that your impact will become unquantifiable.

I can hear you now: How do I get started?
Well, I'm glad you asked ☺

Identify Your Skillset

Have you ever seriously pondered your primary skill set? You may even have more than one skill set but one will usually resonate more than the others. Maybe you're a good listener, or mechanically inclined, technologically savvy, creative, charismatic, or patient with children. Maybe your skill set is inherent in the way you process information or your unique view on presenting dilemmas. Once you identify your skill, begin to drill down and list various ways you can apply your skill. If you're mechanically inclined, the floodgates are literally open to you.

You intuitively see how things work, you think non-linearly, you're good with tools and machinery, you're adept at taking things apart and fixing them, and you literally see what others cannot. Think cars, engines, aircraft, helicopters, ships, inventions, and computers. These are only basic starting point ideas from someone who is not mechanically inclined (me), so imagine the gold mine you can come up with when you start brainstorming with other like-minded folks.

Now, drill down even more; identify the population you want to help. At this point you can either consider volunteering to find the right fit for you, clearly identifying a specific company you want to work for that services the particular population you want to help, or deciding whether you'll create a nonprofit or for-profit business. When you are aligned with your natural capabilities and use them in a manner that enriches your life solely by virtue of enriching the lives of others, then you will be living a deliberate life. Then you'll understand what it is to have meaning in your life, real meaning outside of the bubble you currently live in. And as you branch out and collaborate with others, you'll understand that you took what was an ordinary ability and turned it into a superpower by enhancing the lives of others. Anyone can be self-focused and feel justified, but not everyone knows how to win at life. Now you do.

When you live a life of purpose, the byproduct is that you are happier, more creative, and spiritually filled with real substance, and these lead to living a longer, healthier life. This is what you call designing your own destiny. By living a longer, healthier life you enhance the lives of those you directly interact with and you positively influence generations that aren't even born yet. Talk about the power of leverage!

Our minds become clearer and sharper when we write out our ideas on paper. I have several notebooks. I'm constantly writing. It helps me cultivate clarity in my mind. It's how I bring my dreams to life. Write your own dreams on paper and begin today creating a plan. Keep it top of mind. If we keep our thoughts pent up in our head they will inevitably overwhelm us and thwart our ability to strategize appropriately. It's important to write them out! I cannot emphasize this enough.

Find someone you can discuss your ideas with. This sometimes can be a tricky endeavor. I've found in my own life that most of my peers could not relate to my vision because it was my vision, not theirs. This left me feeling frustrated from a lack of creative feedback I so desperately needed. I wanted synergetic brainstorming partners and more often than not, I ended up feeling like I had just watched a movie with a bad ending. Disappointed. Depleted. Disheartened. All I could do was go back to my pen and paper and write it all out again. I later learned nothing becomes dynamic until it is written out again and again and again..........and again.

Get to Work

The formula is not very complicated.
- Have a heart to serve God by serving others
- Identify your skill sets
- Visualize your dream
- Believe in yourself and the power of miracles
- Write out your plan
- Get to work

Well, how do we get to work? *We get to work!*

This is probably the largest area of delay for mankind. Something so simple as *get to work bringing your dream into reality* can stump people for decades. Why?

> Because the mind complicates things.
> Because we think big picture and become overwhelmed.
> Because we're procrastinators, disbelievers, prone to negative thoughts.
> Because we need someone to hold our hand, just until we're not so scared anymore, and more often than not, no one is there to hold our hand.

The truth is there are many reasons, but today we are solution-focused people, so we're mainly interested in the solution. Are you ready for it? Repeat Nike's motto: Just Do It! That's the answer to everything! Now blend a little bit of Oprah's wisdom in there: Just take the next right step. That's all you need to do: Everyday, take the next right step and just do it! This philosophy reduces any complications we can create for ourselves in our busy little minds. In essence, what you are doing is using your natural abilities (regular power) to assist the lives of others (superpower) one step at a time, everyday of your life.

Imagine who you are going to become and the amazing things you will accomplish! Let that excite you! Life is a game; play it! You now know the rules. Take the next right step and just do it!

7

The Superpower of Using What Ails You to Advance You

"Self-pity is our worst enemy and if we yield to it, we can never do anything wise in this world."
~ Helen Keller

One of the great ways to live an empowered and fulfilling life is to turn your problems into a perpetuating sense of purpose and meaning. Whatever ails you in life can be turned against itself to benefit you instead of allowing it to diminish your life. How? By making it the focus of your contribution to society. That's how you mitigate its power.

To ail means to be in pain and who amongst us has experienced pain? We all have! And, we will continue to because we are human; it's part of the package deal we did not sign up for. The reality is while some are born luckier than others; none of us can escape our own dose of life struggle. The range of ailments are vast from having everything in the world you could possibly want yet lacking the love and attention of your parents to being born with no arms or legs, or even worse. Everyone has their own story and every story has value. If we're able to listen with compassionate ears and an open heart, and actually *see* people when we look at them, we allow ourselves to be better positioned to notice the miraculous opportunity for love before us. Although our ailments are different, our pain is not, and neither is our opportunity to use it to advance our lives and the lives of others.

Some people want to know you're relatable; others want you to share some of your experiences so they can see they are not alone in their own. The secret is to make your ailment your superpower by not brooding over it but rather surrendering it to God in order to dominate it. Circumstances are what they are. What are your weapons against your ailment?

Your will and your perspective.

What's your perspective? To use what ails you to advance you. How? By not letting your ailment be your life sentence and not allowing it to control you. This is the journey we must conquer for ourselves.

The irony of life is that what often appears to be an advantage for one person can become the eventual cause of their demise, and what appears to be a disadvantage for another can very well be the one thing that sets them free. This perspective is the fundamental principle of turning what ails you into your superpower. You must change your perspective of what threatens the quality of your life because it is our individual perspectives that create our realities. This is not to suggest the minimization of anyone's life circumstances, but rather to give hope to those being consumed by a sense of defeat. There are many suffering in this way irrespective of what socioeconomic environment they were born into because suffering is subjective. A gift is only a gift when it is recognized as such and can only be turned into a superpower when used to benefit another.

Miracles ARE Possible

Miracles are possible when we believe. Often times we miss our miracles and the gifts of life because humanity suffers from self-identifying with what all is wrong in our lives, but I warn you, that is a trick against our minds. It is by learning to control your mind that you're then able to reframe your circumstances in a manner that allows you to find the sparkle of hope within any avalanche of darkness that attempts to prohibit you from seeing clearly. From this sparkle we are able to see the light that awaits our recognition, which can lead us to a path of freedom. Thomas Paine said, "We learn the real man smiles in trouble, gathers strength from distress, and grows brave by reflection". Maybe you find it difficult to smile in the face of trouble because it requires faith but faith is what we must muster: faith in our creator, faith in ourselves, faith in our capabilities, faith in miracles, and faith in possibility. Faith is the life preserver that keeps us afloat until we learn how to reflect with the Holy Spirit.

How do we gain strength from distress? By not looking at our circumstances through human understanding, but by using our faith to reveal opportunity in that which tries to impede our growth. There is always opportunity lurking in the shadow. Those without faith cannot see it because they see with their emotion and logic. You must see from your spirit.

Very rarely will life hand us an untethered footing because the purpose of life is to challenge our survivability. It is incumbent upon us to figure out the best perspective to adopt in order to weather the storm and produce our own rainbow for which no cloud can diminish. Here in lies the secret to your superpower. Here is where you must have relationship with your creator to understand your human experience differently.

Mr. Payne stated that man grows brave by reflection and it is within this dimension that we are able to increase the light from the sparkle, which then will open a new path for us to champion, and champion we must. Time does not consider the pro nor the con; it simply continues to pass. You and only you have the power to maximize your superpowers by using what ails you to advance in life, or else you will slowly perish. This choice is your birthright. No one can take it away from you. You have the blessing of wisdom of those who have come before you to help empower your ability to dominate that which threatens your livelihood. They are called mentors.

The Better Version of You

My first mentor was Jesus. Like Jesus, I have not personally met most of my mentors, but rather I learned of their wisdom through books and biographies on YouTube and in blog posts. There is no shortage of courage in the world to borrow from. There is no corner of trouble you cannot turn away from, but it must begin with a decision – a decision from within the depths of your soul to acknowledge, "Yes, that which ails me may not be fair but I can surely conquer it for it is no match for me". How do we know this? Because we have faith in the Word of God and it tells us that no weapon formed against us shall prosper!

There are sad stories of people who ail in every town and in every city across the globe but your soul must proclaim it will not perish. To perish without an intelligent battle from what ails you is dishonorable. There is a better version of you not yet witnessed that needs you to be strong so it can be birthed. You have yet to meet the better version of you. You have yet to meet the best version of you: the warrior, the alchemist, the one who understands what can come from faith the size of a mustard seed when blended properly with indomitable grit and determination. You do not have the right to feel sorry for yourself because there are people in the world worse off than you. Reduce the volume of your whimpering and turn your sight to your creator. Your mind will cry out as a raging fire, your body will want to give up, your eyes will have you believe there is no other possible option, and still you must believe.

You Owe This Child

Have you met the child who will come after you looking for hope from someone with your exact story? It is you that will unknowingly save their life. Your suffering and your fight will not be in vain. All that you will do will work toward helping humanity avoid their own minefields and pitfalls, which are setup to wipe them off the face of the earth, but you will not allow it because your soul knows it must be victorious over that which plagues humanity. You are not alone. You are amongst the heroes you have never met. You will be victorious. You must be because we need more heroes in this land. Do not be another whimpering complainer full of sobbing despair proliferating your grief and infecting the spirits of others. Subdue your natural instinct to feel sorry for yourself for surely there is another worse off than you who conquers in this moment. They know they must because they, too, refuse to perish.

Use what ails you to embark on a conquest for others. They need your example; they need your light. Many have gone before you to be your example. Borrow strength from their victory and dare not allow the enemy to confuse your ability for you are a child of the most-high God. If you must perish in agony at least perish while in battle to save your life. Do not succumb to the negative, invisible energy in your mind. It's not real. Rebuke it!

Think of Bethany Hamilton whose arm was bitten off by a shark. One month later, she got back on her surfboard and two years later won 1st place in the National Scholastic Surfing Association Championship. Or Oprah who gave birth at 14 years old after being raped by a family member only to lose her child to illness but went on to become the 1st African American woman billionaire. Or Kris Carr, another American hero who turned the treachery of cancer that tried to literally kill her into a business of hope and healing for those who needed a light to guide them, and picked up NY Times #1 best selling author in the process. Franklin D. Roosevelt became paralyzed at 39 years old yet went on to win governor of New York and led the country as our 32nd president. He also became the only president to serve for more than two terms, and the man could not even walk.

There's also me, Dr. Cruz, once just a little frightened girl gravely mistreated in foster care and followed throughout her life by the shadow of death. One fateful night, as my abuser held me down and threatened my daughter, I was forced to look the devil in his eyes and the reflection of my reality jolted my consciousness. The threat was so palpable that I realized I had lived in fear for 37 years of my life and that night would be the last of those nights. The next day, I began Designing my own Destiny.

So you see, there is no shortage of ordinary people who have kicked their ailments in the ass and used the lessons learned to advance their lives and the lives of others. Trust me, it can be done!

No Arms or Legs

Two of my personal heroes who set me straight instantaneously when I'm having a bad day are Nick Vujicic and Kyle Maynard. Neither of these men have arms or legs. As far as their physical bodies go, they only have a torso and a head, yet they have more heart than you or I put together! Kyle has climbed Mount Kilimanjaro without the aid of prosthetics and Nick has traveled to more than 57 countries inspiring fully functional people with his amazing life story. Despite not having any limbs, this man paints, swims, skydives, drives, and surfs. How can that be? You must research that answer out on your own.

So I beseech you, look deep within your soul and find the sparkle of hope that awaits you. Then look around the world and actually see the people who need you to win so they can gain hope for themselves. Your testimony will make this world a better place for everyone, even generations not yet born.

8

The Superpower of a Financial Goal

"Money is only a tool. It will take you wherever you wish, but it will not replace you as the driver."

~ Ayn Rand

You need more money. Everyone does. Those who say they do not are lying to themselves. If someone you love could only be saved by what money can buy, like expert medical care, would you then admit you need more money? This is a real possibility for us all. More money means healthier food, cleaner water, air, living in a safer community, and better opportunities for our children. Who doesn't want to provide their children and grandchildren better opportunities? Everyone wants better for their family. The problem is people don't always know what to do to live better. I know I didn't for many years until I started reading personal growth and development books and watching YouTube videos and seminars by Jim Rohn, Bob Proctor, Les Brown, Zig Ziglar, Tony Robbins, which has now evolved into Gary Vaynerchuk, Grant Cardone, Tai Lopez, and Coach Burt.

So the question becomes, "How do you get more money". The answer is you must either sell a product, offer a service, or find another way to earn positive cash flow. These options open the door to unlimited opportunities. The only challenge any of us truly have is in actually dreaming big enough. Are people creative enough to come up with their own ideas? Usually not, and that's why mentorship is so important.

Do you have a mentor? If your answer is no, you probably won't generate much extra income. If your answer is yes, then you probably will. We were not made to live in isolation, nor can we make money in isolation. Technology is advancing too quickly. The market has already developed the first flying car. Did you know that? Yeah! So, if they can make flying cars, don't you think you can figure out one way to generate extra income?

Ways to Generate More $$$

You can sell t-shirts, bake goods, sew something, join a network marketing group, invest in real estate, or become licensed in a trade and open your own side business. You can also Google 100 ways to earn extra income. You can babysit, tutor, collect other people's junk and sell it. You can even sell stuff you don't use in your own house. You can start a lawn maintenance business, sell your drawings, paintings, fashions, sell your music, or start any other kind of business and begin to build it up!

As you make extra money, I recommend reinvesting at least 50% back into your business and save 40%. Yes, that means you only get to spend 10% until you buy your first asset that makes you cash flow every month. Your job now is not only to figure out how you're going to generate more income, but what you're going to invest it in to make extra cash flow. Now would be a good time to start really digging in and gaining knowledge. If you've been watching T.V. for 3-5 hours after school or work, now would be the right time to start using 2-4 of those hours working on advancing yourself in a side hustle. No one can create your destiny but you. You need to get dedicated to the cause, motivated to leave a legacy, and focused on becoming the super star of your family for this generation in order to inspire the next.

It's time. Take out some paper and list all your talents, skills, and abilities. Then Google 100 ways to earn extra income. Santa is not going to manifest the gift for you and Superman isn't going to come save you. It's time you gave a damn about going the extra mile. It's time to figure out how you can earn extra money and turn it into a career that can literally make you millions. It's time to challenge yourself. Get out of your comfort zone. What will this mean for your family? How can this potentially save your children one day? Dream the big dream! It's the only way to gain the momentum required to achieve the dream. Decide right now what your new financial goal is, then add a zero to it!

9

The Superpower of Thinking Assets

"Assets put money in your pocket, whether you work or not, and liabilities take money from your pocket."
~ Robert Kiyosaki

What is an asset? An asset is anything of value that can be converted into cash, which produces value. Examples of assets include mutual funds, stocks, annuities, cash value life insurance policies, CDs, real estate, government securities, commercial paper, buy-sell agreements, distribution rights, broadcast licenses, easements, manuscripts, royalty agreements, use rights of air, water, land, consumer goods, musical compositions, artwork, patents, etc. This list is not all-inclusive and some will have better returns than others. Do your research.

The important thing to remember about assets is that they make you money. Don't get overwhelmed with the list. Pick one and get started. Keep it simple. Start a savings account for yourself and save your extra income until you have enough money to invest in something that will generate you more income then your savings account because savings accounts are probably the worst asset you can have, but it's useful when you're starting off. The goal is not to stay there.

Robert Kiyosaki has a cash flow game I highly recommend and last I heard it's free online. I have the actual game board at home and I play it with my family. It has taught each of us to "think assets". Don't overlook the value of building a home library. Not one of solely sci-fi books but of those that will increase your personal growth and development: books on financial literacy, real estate, geography, communication skills, neuroscience, psychology, influence, confidence, leadership, and of course the classic Think and Grow Rich by Napoleon Hill, Rich Dad Poor Dad by Robert Kiyosaki, anything by Maxwell Maltz, Bob Proctor, Tony Robbins, Grant Cardone, and of course me,

Capri Cruz. We will help you keep your mind sharp and ahead of this game called life. We will keep you focused on "thinking assets" and the skills needed to obtain them.

Encourage the love of reading in your home at an early age and start by reading to your children while they're still in the crib. The library you build today will help you design your destiny and will replicate the same gift to your children as they grow and develop. I encouraged you to print a "Think Assets" sign, frame it and hang it up somewhere visible in your home as an everyday reminder so you and your children will remember the importance of building wealth.

Avoid a Lack of Assets in Your Future

I'm always curious how it is that people in their 50s, 60s, and 70s are so financially disadvantaged. Take for instance the 50-year-old. Let's say he worked from the age 30-50 for a total of 20 years at an average of $40,000 a year. He would have made $800,000 during that time period. If you ask him at age 50 what he has to show for all of those long hours working away from his loved ones, what do you think he will say? Probably that he has a home he does not own out right, a car that he's still paying on or that is old and has seen its better days, he has credit card debt, possibly student loans, and if he's lucky, a small retirement fund of probably about $60,000. How can that be? Where the hell did $800,000 go and how is it at 50 years old so many people have so few, if any, assets generating income for them.

Well, what happened is no one taught them to think in terms of assets and instead they probably had 2-4 children, which is the most expensive responsibility of a person's life costing anywhere from $230K-$500K per child. This number includes day care fees, school clothes, school lunches, school supplies, extra curricular activities, field trips, prom, lawyers and court fees during their terrible teens, college tuition, tutors, medical insurance, braces, hair products, a car, a wedding, spring break, 25 birthdays, 25 Christmases, and all the other miscellaneous needs they will have. Now multiply that $230K -$500K by 2, 3, or 4 children. It's nothing short of crazy. Having children is the quickest way to stay broke. Yes, we love our babies but they are definitely not considered a financial asset. If people are going to have children and want any kind of financial wealth for their future, it's best if they wait to have children until after they have acquired some assets to generate ongoing income.

What else consumes people's incomes over their lifetime? Walmart, cars, medical insurance, make up, expensive services such as weaves, extensions, and other regularly scheduled hair appointments, designer clothes, electronics, and general frivolous spending. If we do not talk to our children very early in life about buying assets, it's likely not to be a conversation we will ever have with them, and if by some chance we do have the conversation with them it may be just a little too late. Even beginning an investment purchase at the age of 30 will have cost the owner 10 years of lost compounded interest that they can never regain because those years are gone. We cannot get time back so creating a family culture of Thinking Assets needs to be purposefully cultivated within the home immediately.

Instead of having newspapers lying around, consider going to the library and asking for some free financial magazines and leave them lying around the living room for your children to see over the years as they grow up. Instead of worrying about them taking classes in school that will have no value in their future, consider teaching them how to start a business, balance a checkbook, understand tax forms in order to maximize their deductions, invest in real estate, and acquire income generating assets.

Instead of buying them $1K of truly worthless junk at Christmas why not use ¾ of that money and open up an investment account for them, even before they're born. Encourage your children to purchase their first rental property by the age of 22. Just by suggesting it you will increase your child's awareness level of its importance. There are many 22-year-olds who own rental property. When parents raise their children to think in terms of assets and liabilities, the culture within the home creates an atmosphere conducive to that level of growth. It is very likely they can become multimillionaires in this generation. Teach them how to use their profits to advance society. Some fund medical research, contribute to end world hunger, build water filtration systems in 3rd world countries, and provide housing for homeless foster care alumni. Develop the minds of your children to love wealth building and philanthropy as early as possible so they can begin designing their destinies in this way.

10

The Superpower of Your Doppelgänger

"Whichever version of "you" you decide to become, already exists."
~ Dr. Capri Cruz

There is a world available to us all within our minds that many are unaware of and thus, do not leverage. It's the place of creativity, possibility, imagination, and it's the same place that as a kid we had a great time, which provided a world of pretend, only it wasn't really pretend to us, was it? As a child it was real, more real than our parents reality. And who's to say which one was actual reality when we all lived in the world we acknowledged. As children we were very happy there. Wasn't that our reality? Yes, it was. Our parents on the other hand lived in what they deemed their reality, and honestly they weren't as happy as we were, were they?

Well, this world of pretend extended from a place within our minds called our imagination and in that place sometimes live imaginary friends with whom we had a great time. They were as real to us as if they were sitting right next to us playing with our toys. We even had full-fledged conversations with them, some were our most trusted confidants.

As adults, there is in extension to this field of imagination that houses someone called your doppelgänger. A doppelgänger is in apparition of you. In fact, there are countless doppelgängers in the land of your imagination and their purpose is to help you become who it is you want to become. Whatever version of yourself you can imagine, there is a doppelgänger waiting to counsel you on the path to becoming. All you have to do is believe it exists and visit it in your mind.

Different Versions of Yourself

Your doppelgänger is actually you. It's just a different version of you. Currently you are the version of you that you are but 10 years ago you were a different version of yourself, right? Yes. And in 1, 5, 10, 15 years from now you will be a different version of yourself than you are right now. Well, if you'd like to take greater control over the version you will become, you can sit quietly, begin meditating, calm your physiology down, and enter into the world of your imagination. This is the same place that Steve Jobs visited before coming up with his inventions, as did Walt Disney and Albert Einstein. Every person visits their imagination before they create something. Every person who uses the technique of visualization visits this place of unknown time deep within the space called our imagination.

The capacity of your imagination is another one of your superpowers and by using it you can see through your mind's eye any variation of you that you wish to see. Would you like to meet the lawyer version of yourself? The public speaker, real estate investor, multimillionaire who lives in

Bel Air, world renowned singer, chef, police chief, fashion model, the amazing father you will become, the firemen, or social media superstar. All you have to do is decide whom you want to talk to and your doppelgänger will appear.

Why is this significant? Because you can leverage this power to consult with your doppelgänger and make them a part of your mental mastermind group. If you want to become a lawyer, for instance, who better to ask for guidance than the version of you who is already a lawyer. You will change your entire life if you embrace your doppelgänger. You can see yourself living in an advanced state of existence in order to gain inspiration and borrow confidence not yet developed in the current version of you.

Who Do You Want to Meet?

Do you want to see yourself giving a kick ass speech? Going into your mind and meet the award-winning 6-figure motivational speaker version of yourself and learn his or her techniques. Do you want to meet the version of you who plays the violin in the New York Philharmonic Symphony orchestra or the gold medalist gymnast? How about the New York Times #1 Best-Selling author, or the CEO of your own nonprofit? Who do you want to become? What version of you do you want to meet? What wisdom would you like to gain from your doppelgänger?

You can ask your doppelgänger:

- What steps to take to achieve your desired goals.
- How did you become so happy?
- How did you publish your book?
- How did you become so self-confident?
- What steps you should take next in life?
- How to trust yourself?
- How to become more courageous?

And literally anything else that comes to your mind. Whatever you need to know to create your ideal existence lives inside your mind and your doppelgänger will reveal it to you. This technique is a superpower that can catapult you life in a way that surpasses other people because most are unaware of its existence and clueless how to leverage it.

11

The Superpower of
Being the Cheetah, Not the Gazelle

"What are you?" I said irritably. In the Serengeti, Ms. Lane, I would be the cheetah. I'm stronger, smarter, faster, and hungrier than everything else out there. And I don't apologize to the gazelle when I take it down."
~ Karen Marie Moning

One hot summer day in sub-Saharan Africa there lay a cheetah in the grasslands looking out into the field. Just beyond its edge there stood a gazelle. The cheetah leaped from his hind legs and hit max speed of 70 mph in just three seconds. Outperforming the Porsche, the cheetah glided through the air by way of 21-foot strides and the flexibility of his elastic spine in the propulsion of almost bionic muscles, this cheetah never took his eyes off of his prey.

His prey is his goal.

The cheetah sees nothing but his goal right in front of him. The cheetah does not doubt, hesitate, pause, or relax in its approach. The cheetah takes flight through leaps and bounds powered by its hunger, desire, instinct, and birthright. It nearly flies in pursuit with precision of target.

Any one of the 19 species of gazelles in Africa are light on their feet and can reach up to 60 mph, as well, in order to escape its predator. The problem for the gazelle is it's always the prey and never the predator. The gazelle spends most of his life walking around aimlessly in wide-open areas where he is easily targeted. He browses the grass most of the day, which means their head is down unaware of its surroundings. The cheetah always has the advantage of attack. The cheetah is equipped not only with physical power but intense focus, determination, and the ability to patiently stalk its prey before executing an offensive attack. The cheetah is always crystal clear of its goal: to dominate!

What About You?

Do you have a goal? How long have you stalked it out? Have you contemplated how you will move forward in your progress? Have you sized up what you see before you in your mind's eye, as well as that which is in your heart? Do you feel it in your bones? Has it consumed your instincts like that of the cheetah? Can you commit to being a cheetah and attacking your goals with the fervor of a wild animal protecting his family with focus, strength, and speed? Success loves speed.

Can you make a move tonight? What can you do? How can you take on the qualities of a cheetah right now in your own life? Can you be relentless, fearless, and calculating? Can you lock your concentration on the prize before you and never blink? Can you execute a 21-foot leap with your elastic spine and sprint into action immediately? Can you be disciplined and committed? Or will you be the gazelle, always running away from that which is determined to devour it? How long will you complain about the misery in your life before realizing you are being the gazelle? How long will you complain about the job or co-workers who make you miserable? How long will you complain about Uncle Sam taking his cut before you learn to out earn your own complaints? How long will you tolerate the unhealthy relationship you are in because you're scared to be alone? How long are you going to try and convince yourself that the work to stay is easier than the work to leave? How long will you remain a victim? How long are you going to be the fragile gazelle in your own life?

All That Is Required

Success and happiness are there for the proclaiming and taking. It will not walk up to your door and knock so you can invite it in. No, you must be the cheetah and know what it is you're focused on and then work your ass off like your life depends on it in order to achieve it.

No more no less. Bleed from your eyes before being the gazelle.

Pure intense predatory gaze into the depths which is your prey, pre-contemplative calculation, combined with the strength of a cheetah in mid-sprint with the persistence of victory looming ahead. All there is and all there ever can be is you (the cheetah) and your prey (your goal).

Do not delay.

Do not hesitate.

Do not flinch.

Do not second-guess it.

Go after that which your spirit reveals is your calling. There are others in the world who need you to be bold, courageous, and stand out from everyone else. You have exactly what they need! Make them your priority and you will be motivated to achieve your goal. Action is the name of the game. Put in the work and gain your reward. Own your birthright like the cheetah and attack your goals!

12

The Superpower of Refusing to Fail

"When you refuse to fail, you play a very different game."
~ Dr. Capri Cruz

Somewhere between serving 20 years on active duty service in the U.S. Navy and 20 years of being a single mother, I adopted the attitude that success was my only option in life. I recall hearing that phrase in one of Eminem's songs and I hung on to it for dear life because the potential for failure was everywhere I was. I could feel it. I had felt it for many years but I lacked a clear vision of the opposing forces that surrounded me. Still, I sensed it because I was intuitively aware of the lack of control I felt over my own life and I didn't like it. "Success is my only option" became my life's mantra. I typed it in 3-inch letters on a sheet of paper and taped it to my computer. This little sign became my saving grace because in my weakest moments it reminded me that I would never fail. The more I focused on success being my only option the more I refused to fail!

Negative spirits surrounded me. These people were evil. I felt the ranks were closing in on me. I had become someone's target. Their energy was down right hateful and I had no escape except the escape I found within my mind. The truth was I never knew about my superpowers specifically that of preparation and deliberate creation, so I felt I could not change my circumstances. I had allowed myself to end up in a situation where I had very little control over my own life. I was, in essence, a prisoner of my mind. Fear wrecked havoc in my mind. I was very well aware that I was the low man on the totem pole, not only at work but also in my own life. I had not learned of my personal powers. The consequence was I allowed my life to be at someone else's mercy, and I hated that. Still, there was nothing I could do about it, or so I thought.

Something Amazing Happens When...

As time passed an internal mindset come over me that was rooted in this declaration that not only was success my only option, but with every ounce of life in my body, I refused to fail. ~I refused to fail! ~ I refused to fail. ~ I REFUSED to fail! I recall saying that I was going to kick life's ass just as soon as I could because I was done with it kicking mine. I didn't realize that by adopting these two philosophies: Success is my only option and I REFUSE to fail, I was already kicking life's ass. With that kind of mindset, there's not a whole lot life can do to you anymore. I thought I was still on the receiving end. I did not realize I was the one dishing out the orders.

Something amazing happens when you REFUSE to fail. You develop grit. You develop a snarl. You turn into a tough son-of-a-bitch. Say it with me, "I REFUSE to fail." Now say it with a Brooklyn attitude. "I REFUSE to fail!" That mindset has a different affect than does "Success is my only option." Both are powerful, just in different ways. Used together, you now have yourself a new superpower, my friends. Refusing to fail gives you the extra strength, focus, endurance, and posture needed to level up. "I REFUSE to fail" means you can hit me with all you got and I will still rise. I REFUSE to let you own me. I REFUSE to let you kick my ass. You Sir, will die before I fail. Nothing and no one can ever say or do anything that will keep you down when you REFUSE to fail. Your indomitable focus will penetrate their feeble existence.

REFUSE to fail! Get up, climb, push through with endurance, make sure your great grandchildren will be prou of you. REFUSE to fail. Your fight is not in vain. REFUSE to fail. No excuses. No bullshit stories. No rationalization. No reasons or explanations. Just pure BEAST MODE! Say it, "I REFUSE to fail!" It takes HEART. Do you have HEART? No matter your struggle, REFUSE to fail. You are putting the ether on notice that you are no match for its attempt to steal your livelihood. It's impossible because you livelihood is in your mind; a place no one has access. Your blood, your sweat, your tears; no matter what army stands before you, no matter how out numbered you are, no matter the manpower that attempts to intimidate you, no matter the beast that threatens your life – REFUSE TO FAIL!

The Strength of Refusing

Your mind will become a bed of nails to guard against those who dare attempt to infiltrate your thoughts. Nothing will destroy you. Nothing will even come close because your armament is your REFUSAL. There in lies your superpower, my friend. Do you know how strong a refusal is? When someone refuses to do something, there's no negotiation, there's no discussion, there's no interest in a joint or group effort for anything. You simply refuse. You are now as strong as a 16-inch impenetrable steel door that shuts in the face of threat and adversity. There is no more listening, caring, slowing down, taking into account or tolerating. It's just not going to happen. It's over. You REFUSE. You will no longer take anything else into consideration. It just doesn't exist. Say it with me and say it with attitude, "I REFUSE to fail". BOOM! Case closed.

Got it?

Ok, great! That's F'n outstanding! I'm very proud of you. Now breathe. Feel your chest lower as you relax. Allow your blood pressure to stabilize. You are now playing on offense. Defense is a loser's game. Now that we got that straight, what's next for you? Well, refusing to fail must transition from a mantra to a mentality that gets imbedded into your DNA. You must live and breathe it with certainty. This mentality of REFUSING to fail must fuse itself into your core beliefs as a human being. It can't just be something cute you say to sound tough. It must be real for you on a molecular level.

As you shift focus to narrow in on your life goals and the strategies needed to achieve your goals, you must have this knowing in your bones that you are BAD ASS. Success is your only option! And you REFUSE to fail! And even though you may not have all your ducks in a row yet, you know in due time you will because that's the path you're now pursuing. This is what warriors are made of. ~ Honor ~

Can you feel it inside of you yet? You are now armed with two of the most impenetrable pieces of armor known to man.

What do you fear now?
NOTHING!

When failure is no longer an option, you know it has changed the shape and color of the lens from which you see life. No longer are there moments of self-pity. There is only feedback from the universe telling you you've either made a wrong turn or you hit a detour and need to recalculate your direction. It's okay to take a knee when life gets tough, but baby, you better get back up and REFUSE to fail!

13

The Superpower of Molding Your Life to Your Will

"Your life is your own. You mold it. You make it. All anyone can do is to point out ways and means, which have been helpful to others. Perhaps they will serve as suggestions to stimulate your own thinking until you know what it is that will fulfill you, will help you to find out what you want to do with your life."
~ Eleanor Roosevelt

After having lived a life of mental and physical imprisonment for decades, I've been chosen by some universal mysticism to share the secrets of life with you. I need you to pay very close attention because if you can grasp this truth you will have the solution to every problem you will ever have. It's so powerful that I consider it modern-day magic and I, myself, use this concept to mold life to my will. Would you like to mold life to your will? Take a moment and think about that because if you will accept the idea that life can be molded to your will, what would your life look like? What changes would you make? What would you incorporate? What would you improve? Remove?

Hear me and hear me well. Life IS moldable to your will because life as you know it is birthed from your beliefs, it exists in your mind and is reflected back to you in your perspective. Stop here for three seconds and breathe that in. Repeat it. "My life is a reflection of my perspective". Your life is a reflection of your perceptions. What you perceive is a representation of what you believe. Your thoughts are what create your experiences.

Now it's important to understand that in the physical world everything you perceive lives in a time-space dimension, which means it takes time to change certain physical representations in your life. For instance, if you want a new home it will take time to mold your life in the way it needs to be molded for that now to show up, but what can and will change in a split second, if you allow it, is the reality that is represented in your mind by your perceptions. Are you getting this? The power to mold, change, alter, or otherwise create the reality you want for your life resides in your mind.

Your Brain vs Your Mind

At this point, a noteworthy distinction to understand is that your mind is not your brain. Your brain is a physical organ made up of tissue that weighs approximately 2 to 3 pounds. That is not your mind. Your mind is not a physical thing you can touch. For discussion purposes, let's narrow down the understanding of the mind to the universal power that lives within each human being that generates thoughts. When thoughts are accepted and programmed into the subconscious mind then thoughts become beliefs.

The power to mold your life according to your will by believing in the philosophy that all of life first exists in your mind is not purely an academic point. It's a fundamental belief to be accepted or rejected as a basic existential principle in order to harness its inherent power. If you accept the belief it will work for you. If you reject the belief, it will not, and here in lies the reason why some people's lives are filled with marvelous sensations and others are not. Your physical world is a direct reflection of your inner perspective, which creates your vibrational frequency. Life as you know it exists in your mind. Once you understand this power you will also understand that if you want something in your life to change it must first be changed in your mind. Let's look at some examples:

- Do you hate your job? It's a perception.
- Do you feel ugly? It's a perception.
- Do you feel stuck in life? It's a perception.
- Are you poor? It's a perception.
- Do you feel powerless? It's a perception.

- Do you feel you can't make more money? It's a perception.
- Do you get intimidated easily? It's a perception.
- Do you feel powerful? It's a perception.
- Can you achieve greatness? It's a perception.
- Can you be unaffected by other people's negativity? It's a perception.

Every thought that exists in your mind is a perception. Whose mind? Your mind. If it's your mind and it's your perception then guess who has the power to change it?

Life Exists in Your Mind First

Stay focused on this point: All of life exists in your mind, so in order to change your life you need to first change your mind. That means your thoughts, perceptions, and beliefs. Your entire paradigm. This is a basic fundamental pillar for change. It is not all-inclusive, meaning if you want to change something concrete in your life, yes, there are other elements that need to be included for it to come to fruition such as execution, but not until the change in your mind first occurs. You must believe in it. For example, if you want to increase your income, yes, you must adopt the belief that its possible first, but then you must also find an income producing activity to initiate and repeat that activity until your desired income is evident in your bank account. But remember, you cannot increase your income if you don't first believe it's possible. Then you can create a plan, a strategy, and execute.

Many people destroy any possibility of a better life before it has a chance of proving itself to be possible because their beliefs tell them they can't achieve certain things. "It's not possible", they tell themselves. Fear, doubt, and extreme risk-aversion magnify the negative. These emotional states are all murders. They kill any possibility of you molding your life to your will.

Do not get distracted by how much time is required for something to come to fruition. This thought will take you off course and reduce your motivation. There is no way for you to determine how long something might take. You can guesstimate based on probability but you cannot predict the power of the universe. The incredible magic created by serendipity, kindness toward others, miracles, chance happenings, coincidences, and other unpredictable manifestations of the universe are always at work and are noticeable when you are in alignment with such beliefs.

Stay focused on the power of your mind. For instance, to feel beautiful does not require a physical change. It requires a new appreciation and a new perspective of the miracle that is you. To feel empowered doesn't require a physical change. A physical change will amplify a sense of empowerment but the possibility of feeling empowered must first occur in your mind. To get unstuck in life does not require a physical change. It requires a vision, which occurs in the mind, and then the follow-through will be new action.

A person can take action to get unstuck in life but if he does not first have the belief system in his mind, no amount of action will fulfill his void. To love people occurs first in the mind. To be kinder, more patient, creative, solution oriented, helpful, a change agent, physically healthier, and literally anything else you can think of must first occur in the mind because your physical world is generated from your mental world. More specifically, your physical world is born from your beliefs. He who believes he can and he who believes he can't are both right.

Can you mold your physical life to your will? Absolutely, because your life is only a representation of your thoughts. Recall the infamous words of William Shakespeare, "There is nothing either good or bad, but thinking makes it so". Thinking is EVERYTHING. Are you beginning to understand the power you have now? This is unequivocally life changing. It is happening every day of everyone's life but most people aren't aware of its occurrence, much less their personal power to control it and yield desired results. When you realize this is your primary superpower your life will become a fun game instead of a burden to endure.

14

The Superpower of Taking Complete and Total Personal Responsibility

"Taking personal responsibility is a beautiful thing because it gives you complete control of your destiny."
~ Heather Schuck

The mere act of taking complete and total personal responsibility for your life is an immediate game changer because most people vehemently resist doing so. This is one of the easiest ways for you to get ahead in life and bypass those who will still be complaining about their pasts long after you have made something amazing of yourself. By taking complete and total personal responsibility for your life you immediately turn an ordinary power into a superpower.

I have to say, it was the primary driver to my initial success in life because it primed my mind for dynamic change. When you decide to live by this type of creed, you no longer allow excuse-making, blaming, and rationalizations to dominate your worldview. You realize it doesn't matter if someone is to blame. It doesn't matter if your rationalizations are true. You recognize those thought processes for what they are, self-defeating, and they become unacceptable because they are the antithesis of your creed.

Many people who struggle with taking full responsibility for their lives do so because so much of their current life conditions are a result of unfortunate formative circumstances. Any of us who have had jacked up childhoods would have to honestly say that yes, we absolutely can find someone to blame for our life struggles. There's always a cause to an effect, and to be quite honest, it's not fair. It's actually fucked up, but the gig is that life doesn't give a shit if it's not fair. Fair is not a rule in this game called life so stop expecting fairness to show up.

Shift Your Mental Focus

When we finally decide that pointing blame will no longer be a part of our personal dialogue, we immediately shift our mental focus from that of being a victim in our lives to being the leader, and maybe a very pissed off leader because life is not fair. Owning the fact that life is not fair is infuriating at first sometimes, and then we get over it and figure out how to WIN! Use your anger and aggression to benefit your progress, not hinder it. This is where we need to move forward smartly with a strategy, not emotionally erratic flying off the handle every time we get a reflection of reality. Instead we need to channel that energy into the execution of our strategy for success. Shift your mental focus from helplessness to empowerment. Shift your mental focus from others to self, and from what you didn't have control over to what you now have control over. Taking complete and total responsibility for EVERYTHING is a game changer.

One thing many people seem to overlook as their anger and pain looms over their mindset is that the amount of power and control they have over their lives will be a byproduct of having control over their mind. Those of us connected to the reality of life realize it's hard for most people to get ahead but it's hard because they are in the energy of experiencing their lives as a recipient of events instead of viewing themselves as the creator of their life experiences and emotions. Making this shift will change everything. Shifting into the mindset of being the creator is where the magic begins.

We are creators of our mindsets.

We are creators of our interpretations.

We are creators of the goals we set for our futures.

We are the creators for the plans we make.

We are the creators of the actions we take.

We are the creators of the images we hold in our minds.

We are the creators of the perspectives we choose to have.

We are the creators of the belief systems we embrace.

We are the creators of who we believe has control over our lives and our futures.

Becoming the Creator

To become this creator in actuality, you must first create the fundamental mindset that you are the creator and hold yourself accountable for annihilating all negative thoughts that arise in opposition to creation. This is where people revert back to old ways of thinking because humans are creatures of habit and we seek the path of least resistance. Let's take for example someone who says their life is the way it is because their parents abandoned them or didn't teach them the fundamentals to have a successful life. Those people, and I once was one of them, are stuck in the historical cause and effect phase of development and they get stuck there because of the anger, blame, resentment, and learned helplessness, which often arises when facing the reflection of their life's reality because we spent so many years just living, we never reflected.

Once we reflect it's far easier to blame others for the consequences we now endure. I didn't create this mess; oh, but we did contribute by being passive in our approach to our future. And yet, we can find someone to blame for that too. So it does us well to stop blaming because it's a hamster wheel we may never get off of otherwise. This is especially true when people have yet to realize that today they have the power to make the needed changes their lives desire despite the "appearance" of their current reality.

We must remember that each person's reality is a result of their ongoing perspectives and once they own the fact that they are the only person responsible for their perspectives and fully commit to taking complete responsibility for changing their interpretations, then they put themselves in the driver seat to move forward smartly realizing their current life is really a gift and an opportunity to evolve. That's the power of perspective. Hear it again: Your current life is really a gift and an opportunity for you to evolve, so use your trials and triumphs to teach yourself and others how to excel in life. This is where your superpower resides.

In my own journey to learning how to Maximize My Superpowers, I proclaimed radical personal responsibility over my life. I shared my perspective with others but they only debated the validity of my philosophy. They tried to disprove it, but it's important to note that they are still emotionally connected to blame. I, by the grace of God, am not. The reason I am not is because I chose to do the work on myself that was needed in order for me to be set free. They chose to be right rather than to seek healthy change. They sought to endorse their own perspective in order to validate their pain, which inhibited their emotional growth. They were more focused on how illogical my philosophy was rather than seeing the potential for transformation.

Become Solution-Focused

One advantage I had that they did not was my training to be solution-focused both in the military and in my profession as a psychotherapist. This is an important distinction because in order to push through life and not allow the proverbial boulders of life to crush us, we must think a certain way. I am fully aware that if I was not a solution-focused person with an orientation toward progressive change, I probably would not have been able to employ the philosophy of taking full responsibility for my past, present, and future. It requires subjugating the ego, lest we continue the cycle of dysfunction.

The essence of my philosophy is that my whole life is my responsibility, which includes my past, present, and future. The people who resisted my philosophy did so primarily because I said I take full responsibility for my past. They could not understand taking responsibility for situations they did not have control over as a child and so they dug their heels in the dirt. Stubbornness and closed mindedness prevailed. Their mindset became paralyzed and was unable to move forward. I completely understood their point but my perspective was if I agreed with them then that opened the door for me to blame others and rationalize details of circumstances, which was only going to waste my time. I was not emotionally attached to my past or present as much as I was to the future I wanted to create for myself. That was the primary distinction between me and those who resisted my philosophy. If I spent one second blaming or rationalizing anything I had experienced in life I would not have been able to advance full throttle like I did.

When I had my awakening at 37 years old, I hit the ground running to make a change. I knew I had already wasted enough time and I wasn't interested in wasting anymore by blaming my dead parents for their mistakes. Because of my research into their upbringings, I realized they were just byproducts of their own dysfunctional parents and therefore, I didn't need to blame them for anything. I found humility and forgiveness for them; consequently, my ability to have compassion for their struggles set me free.

Even one thought about how my current life was the result of someone else's actions would have pacified my complacency, so I did not allow it. Yes, I understood it intuitively but I did not give it life. I just could not allow it to be part of my conversation ever again. It did not matter to me that there was any truth to my life being a domino effect of the actions of those who came before me. That point had no value to me even though I could see the logic in it. I had a choice to make. I could blame and feel justified or I could get on the ball in life and create dynamic changes for those who are alive and depend on me, and for future generations. That's who motivate me. Not dead people who hurt me.

Do You Want to Be Right or Do You Want to Change?

Another distinction between me and those who resisted my philosophy was that they were interested in the premise of logic and I was not. I was interested in change. So for me to bulldoze through life, I had to stay focused on what I was personally responsible for and so I created the philosophy that I was responsible for my entire life: past, present, and future, meaning I was responsible for the interpretation of my past, present, and future because interpretation precedes reality. This philosophy turned my cement boots into wings so I could fly.

Declaring personal responsibility for your entire life puts you in an unrestricted energetic state that allows for radical change. It's a superpower because it catapults you in a way others cannot experience as they're too busy blaming, rationalizing, and thinking logically, always trying to defend their truth, not realizing their so-called truth thwarts their ability to escape their own toxic nature of self-defending. They can't see the forest for the trees. Do yourself a favor, don't be this kind of person. Instead, be open-minded and desire to let go more than you want to hold on.

15

The Superpower of Your Intuition

"Intuition is seeing with the soul."
~ Dean Koontz

Your intuition can be your best friend if you allow it to be. It can be your copilot and your life partner. It has the ability to inform you in a manner that your five senses cannot. According to Merriam Dictionary your intuition is the power or faculty of attaining direct knowledge or cognition without evident rational thought and interference. Researchers have defined intuition as the influence of "nonconscious emotional information" from the body or the brain, such as an instinctual feeling or sensation.

Women's intuition is a popular concept but intuition is not solely accessible by women. Research shows that our intuition is actually part of our instinctual and often unconscious mental processing which is attributed to the prehistoric parts of our brain such as the limbic and reptilia parts of our brain, as opposed to our thinking brain, better known as the prefrontal cortex. Therefore, everyone has intuition. Some believe in it, some do not. If we do not believe in something than it does not exist in our consciousness and therefore cannot be leveraged to assist us in designing our destiny.

How to Know the Unknowable

When we tap into our natural gift of intuition it can help us know the unknowable, know what is not visible to the eye, gain quicker access to wisdom that the thinking mind might take to long to recognize. We can assess situations using our intuition in a manner otherwise not available to us Our focus shifts from an external point of reference to an internal point of reference. Do you think your natural internal state would purposely misguide you? No, it would not. Intuition is an inner awareness that is distinctive from logical processing. It gives you physiological hints (sweaty palms, gut feeling, etc), insights, and an energetic knowing long before your conscious awareness has caught on.

Using your intuition can literally save you years of trouble and regret. It's there to warn you. It's imperative that you lead with intuition because the conscious mind often overlooks warning signs by rationalizing what it wants to believe. According to a research study by neuroscientist Beatrice de Gelder, PhD, intuition is the result of our processing of things that we're not consciously aware of. It's a feeling of knowing that uses an older brain structure but because we're so dependent on our five senses we're not use to trusting our intuitive vision track.

Your Real BFF

Research shows that our instincts often hit us first on a visceral level informing us of information before we're able to consciously assess the situation. By increasing the frequency of your mindfulness practices, you'll more easily pick up your intuitive messages. Your intuition is your best friend. It can instantly inform you whether a person or situation is potentially dangerous, deceitfully sabotaging you, or if you are headed in the wrong direction in life. I suggest you test it out to gain confidence in its service to you. You can do this by having the intention of listening to your gut feelings about people and situations you encounter. Over time gauge whether or not your initial intuitive knowing was accurate.

The evolution of learning to use the unconscious information in your brain will enable you to become more comfortable being intuitively informed prior to making logical decisions. According to a study published in the journal Psychological Science, learning to trust your intuition will allow you to make faster and more accurate decisions. Can you see now why using your intuition is a superpower when compared to those who do not? It often knows what's best for us when our thinking mind has not yet decided.

The thing to remember is that your intuition is instinctual - immediate. Your thinking mind is not. It gets confused with incoming stimuli, old and new belief systems, processing of information, and all the busy work required of a thinking mind. Your intuition lives in the part of your brain that has kept you safe in prehistoric times. Its job is to inform you. Pay attention to it and then process the information for an advantage over those who do not pay it much attention. I assure you, it's your secret weapon.

16

The Superpower of Your Choices

"There are two primary choices in life; to accept conditions as they exist, or accept the responsibility for changing them."
~ Denis Waitley

The power of choice is one of my absolute favorite superpowers because it puts the locus of control within your purview regardless of external circumstances. You always have the power to choose how something will or will not affect you, even when you don't have direct control over your physical environment or experiences in that moment. No one can ever take that ability away from you. It is inherent in you. It is your birthright. Your environment may delay your tangible growth for a time, but the choice to grow or succumb to perceived limitations is a power of your mind and no one has direct access to your mind once you know how to protect it. It's important to note that many people don't know how to protect their mind and they end up feeling like they don't have any power at all, much less the power to make deliberate choices.

Many people unknowingly feel that they are at the mercy of their circumstances but that is a misconception. We have the power to mold life using the power of our perspective, which is a byproduct of our mindset. From that perspective our choices will be determined. We must get to the point of realizing this truth because it's in not knowing this truth that we are held back in life feeling like victims often times not being able to see a way out of our situations. This is why finding yourself some mentors is so important. They can see what you may not be able to.

Why do you think more people aren't aware that the essence of choice is a superpower? Simply put, because no one has taught them. Most parents, I would venture to say, rarely engage their children in conversations about their personal powers and how to use them. Subsequently, children grow up and potentially live for decades unaware of their powers. But once aware, the result of enacting deliberate choice over their lives has the potential for infinite transformational gain.

Give a person a glimpse of their potential for long enough and they will turn that potential into reality.

Activate your Superpower

So how can you begin to exercise this superpower in your own life? Begin small. You can choose to wake up 30 minutes earlier to meditate. You can choose to have specific standards and boundaries for your behaviors toward yourself and others, and the behaviors you'll accept from others. You can choose the types of foods you put into your body. You can choose to stop smoking, get out of an unhealthy relationship, improve your tone of voice when speaking to others, rebuke recognized negative self-talk, arrive to work on time, save an additional 10% of your income for investments, make an additional 10% of income by starting a network marketing business, reduce the amount of hours you watch TV, increase the number of books you read each month, create an enjoyable exercise plan and incorporate it 3-5x a week, choose carefully the thoughts you will accept or reject in order to enhance your future, and ultimately become a contributing member of society. That is the goal in life. Choose to contribute on various levels in order to make a lasting impact in life.

Choose the stories that you will and will not believe about life. Choose to only believe and focus on the stories that empower you. With negative media dominating social media, it's vital that we ditch the racial and political finger pointing, insults, and disrespect, all which diminish our sense of community and personal power. Instead, choose to create more empowering stories that will facilitate your success and advance you toward your fullest potential. Choose to create the life you want to live instead of being wrapped up in the lives of others.

Start by first creating that vision in your mind so that you establish a blueprint. Use this blueprint to create your overall strategy for your life, and follow up with a list of goals that when successfully achieved will fulfill the evolution of your vision. Choose to create strategies. Choose to be happy. Choose an abundant attitude every time! Choose to move the needle of life forward not backward. Choose to live for your dreams, not to avoid anticipated pain. It's smart to be risk-adverse to the extent that you are planning a smart transition out of a less than ideal situation but do not be risk-adverse to the extent that it paralyzes you. Choose to be powerful by being a person of significant value. These are possibilities if you believe in the superpower of choice. It is one of the most powerful superpowers available to you.

The Psychology of Choice

The psychology of choice informs us that when we face too many options it creates a feeling of overwhelm and ultimately produces inaction, also known as choice paralysis. We know choice is a decision we actively or passively make. When we actively make a choice we are more often than not alert that we are making a choice. This doesn't guarantee we are making an intelligent choice as intelligence is based on knowledge gained and applied, but it is a choice nonetheless. To ensure you make an intelligent choice, you must conduct your own research and allow ample time to consider all possible rewards and consequences of such a choice. In either case, the results ultimately affect us on a biological level, so it behooves us to make wise choices. I have learned to appreciate the concept of "sleeping on it" before deciding. The more bad choices we make the greater amount of stress we have to endure. The long-term consequence of stress is physical illness.

When we passively make a choice we may think we're not making an active choice at all, but that's actually a semantical error because to not do something is to actually do something. Understand that when you choose to do nothing you're actually doing something and that something is nothing. So by default you're making a choice even when you decide not to make a choice. There are potential rewards and consequences for doing nothing, as well. Intelligent choice making occurs from the prefrontal cortex of the brain. This part of the brain employs higher-level thinking skills such as rationality, planning, error monitoring, and analytical processing. These executive functions moderate social behavior and contribute to the development of your personality. These are aspects of decision making to consider when deciding what our choices will be because, again, physical illness can result from making poor choices. Poor choices sometimes come as a result of passive choices, those we make in order to avoid that which we may not realize we cannot avoid at all; we actually only delay the inevitable.

The Role of Emotions

Whatever choice we make is always first influenced by our emotions, which is initiated in the middle part of our brain. Many people think they are rational decision-makers first and emotional second but this is not true. We are all first influenced by our emotions as they relate to the object of our decision-making. Then we use our rationality to justify our choice. Remember, we were first emotional beings before we were rational. The delay in rational mature decision-making in our youth stems from the lack of full development of the prefrontal cortex, the thinking brain, until we reach the age of about 25 years old.

Keep in mind, by nature humans prefer the path of least resistance, so success in any realm of your life requires work, which requires self-discipline. Know that you will need to ensure a certain level of self-discipline to achieve a task that requires any significant amount of effort. The probability of you actually accomplishing your life goals increases when you have an accountability partner because they hold you accountable for your choices. When selecting an accountability partner, take into consideration their personal and professional values. The more their values line up with yours, the greater the probability you have made a good choice. The key to keep in mind here is the influence of your "personal preferences" and potential biases, and how they may influence your impending choice. This highlights the need for the decision-maker not to be overtaken emotionally by their personal preferences in lieu of objectivity in order to consider all potential results. This is the basis for good decision-making.

When you are certain that your personal preferences and biases are subjugated by your objective rationality and you have considered the intentional rewards you're attempting to create for your life, then you are in position to declare your choice with a degree of certainty. In doing so, you move your life forward in the direction of your desired result. This is deliberate movement. This is activating your superpower. This is commanding power over your life.

Self-reflect

Take a few moments and analyze the choices you've made in your own life over the years. Make a list on a sheet of paper of what choices were healthy and unhealthy, smart and consequential, and which one's you are proud of and no so proud of. It's important that you learn to be honest with yourself so that you can assess where you can improve. The past only serves you when used as a basis for learning. When you can objectively view your past in this way, you are no longer a prisoner of it. You no longer need to hide, self-medicate, numb yourself to your reality, or self-harm. You are big girls and boys, women and men, with the knowledge that you not only have personal power, but real superpowers. With these personal assets you can now CREATE, not just react or suffer in silence from feelings of shame and helplessness. It's time to have a new attitude about your destiny. This is the destiny you are designing. You must shift into offense mode. You are your own super hero. You are the one who is going to save your own life. You must learn to be truthful with yourself.

After you make the list of your previous life choices that you're proud and not so proud of, take a moment and activate your prefrontal cortex by logically analyzing what is before you. Let's say you quit a job due to an emotional impulse. List the benefits you received from doing that and the consequences. Analyze whether or not there could have been a more beneficial way for you to have achieved the same benefits without the consequences. Ultimately, how could you have made a smarter choice in order to reduce an subsequent suffering? It's important to keep in mind that th is a subjective exercise because those who have low standards for the quality of their lives may not care that the made an impulsive choice.

Those who have higher standards for their quality of life or those driven by guilt may be overly harsh on themselves To hedge against polarizing yourself, just assume you want to live an excellent life and are researching ways to increase the quality of your choices. Once you increase your conscious awareness of the motivating factors of your decision-making, you can choose to train yourself to make smarter, more controlled choices. According to sociologist Martha Beck, "how we do anything is how we do everything", so if your goal is to maximize your superpowers, you must be objective and honest in your evaluation of each superpower in order to gain maximum efficacy of their uses. Trust me, your future self will be glad you did.

Ultimately, the quality of your life will be preceded by the courage you exact in your decision-making. Making good choices is a basic life principle that will be the primary determinant of how your life takes shape, how responsible you become, how much suffering you will endure, how healthy you become, all which adds to or subtracts from your life's longevity. Those who choose to be in domestic violent relationships have a lower life expectancy, so that is not a very good choice to make. A better choice would be how to get out of that relationship and begin surrounding yourself with better quality people so you too can become a better quality person yourself. The path toward improved living always starts with the question "How can I make better choices". Inquiry and self-reflection are the basis of turning an ordinary power into a superpower.

17

The Superpower of Your Voice

"A voice cannot carry the tongue and the lips that gave it wings. Alone must it seek the ether."
~ Kahlil Gibran

Your voice is majestically powerful but its virtue does not automatically make it your superpower. Most people don't yet realize the power of their voice; how to wield it, direct it, use it, or magnify its influence. Just like a construction worker has many tools in his tool belt to get his job done, so do we. Our tools, such as that of our voice, help to maximize the utility of our life. How we use it denotes its actual power.

The power of your voice dwells in your heart, in its projection and consistency, in its refusal to be silenced, and in its wisdom to know when to be silent. It can be transformed and transferred over several mediums. You can share your voice locally with another human being, within groups of people, over radio, television, newspapers, blogs, social media, through prayer, meditation, and through the power of the pen.

You can use your voice to express love, influence a call to action, move people through emotion, and encourage self-reflection. It can express gratitude, empowerment, direction, instruction, inspiration, compassion, desire, creativity, possibility, hope, and admiration. It can move a nation to victory or attempt to justify idiocy. Your voice can give people life or drive them toward death. Your voice is so powerful it can be effective even when it's not being used: the power of silence.

Silence sends a loud and clear message. So does the pause, your tone, pitch, and volume. Did you know a whisper is more powerful than yelling? When you lower your voice you make it so that people must quiet down in order to hear you. You influence the listener to lean in thereby commanding their attention.

Your Power to Influence

If you listen to your own voice when speaking you'll be able to gauge your own physiology, temperament, and emotional state. Psychological research asserts that we have the power to influence or not influence others based on how they perceive our voice. This is an unconscious influence rooted in the listener's subconscious and is revealed by how your voice affects their response. It's also evidenced that women typically find men with deeper voices more attractive and can become sexually aroused by a baritone voice. Don't believe me? Just ask the singers Josh Turner and Shaggy.

Similarly, men are more attracted to certain types of female voices than others. Do men prefer a woman to have a baritone voice or one that sounds more like Marilyn

Monroe's? In a more professional setting, do employees respond better to a mousey voice or one that projects authority? According to Dr. Nick Morgan, one of America's top communication theorists, the undertones of your voice carry your emotions, and therefore, determine how much one person can influence, move, or lead another. The power of your voice is undeniable and once you learn how to activate it as your superpower, you will be well on your way to influencing others and reaping the benefits in your future. The only question left to ask is how can you deliberately use it as your superpower. Well, I'm glad you asked!

Ways to Deliberately Use Your Superpower

The first way is in learning how to control it. Whether in singing, excessive chatter, or hearing it incessantly in your own head, when you learn to control your voice you gain more power over it. Thus, when and how you use it can directly influence the benefit it wields you. This is the ultimate goal of any superpower.

When our desire is to influence an audience, whether on social media or a job interview, we want to ensure we're projecting a powerful, energetic, and confident voice with balance. Your voice can command people or enrapture them into the content of your storyline. If you consciously decide to fall in love with your own voice that will subconsciously improve the quality of your voice and give you more deliberate influence over others because it will reveal greater self-confidence. The more you love your voice, the more you love yourself and that will come across in your communications.

Most people overlook falling in love with their own voice but how do you think young Cassius Clay (later known as Muhammad Ali) turned himself into a gold Olympic medalist? In great part, he loved his own voice and he used it to empower himself and captivate his supporters. He did not hesitate to tell anyone he was the greatest. He used his voice to self-promote and intensify his self-confidence, ultimately imbuing throngs of people with the concept of self-love. His legacy is that of a championship-talker because he knew how to use all facets of his voice. He just might be the best example there is of how to use your voice as your superpower.

God as an Example

Well, on second thought maybe not. God actually has him beat! When you think of the power of God you may recall that all of God's power came from his voice, most specifically in the first six days, according to the Bible. We see evidence of this in Genesis 1:3; "And God said let there be light", and there was light. And again we see in Exodus 3:14 when God said to Moses, "I AM WHO I AM".

If you've ever heard the voice of God resonate within you, you understand it's absolutely, unequivocally a superpower! When you combine your voice with the faith of a mustard seed, surely you will not consider yourself a mere mortal for you possess the power of God within you. Maybe Muhammad Ali knew this. Maybe he knew that what came out of his mouth must not return to him void (Isaiah 55:11), and so he spoke his future into existence. Now it's your turn. How will you use your voice as your superpower?

18

The Superpower of Taking MASSIVE Action

"Knowing is not enough, we must apply.
Willing is not enough, we must do."
~ Johann Wolfgang von Goethe

What's the one thing that evens the playing field for everyone?

Taking action!

There will always be someone smarter, cuter, younger, wiser, more talented, wealthier, or blessed with a more supportive family than you but if that person never takes action, what will they accomplish?

Nothing.

Results require action and "results" happens to be the name of the game. Action is its vehicle. In clearer terms, going to work is the action required to get the result you want: your paycheck. Intelligent calculated action is better than unintelligent uncalculated action, but in most cases some action is better than no action, if we are to become learned people. You just really need to first, consider, and second, try to anticipate the potential consequences and rewards of your actions before taking any action.

Remember the old saying, "Fools rush in". Don't be a fool. The price sometimes can cost you decades. There are times when an ideal situation won't present itself so your decision to act or not to act will boil down to whether or not you're in a good position to absorb the potential consequences. The goal is to stay away from as much consequence as possible but not so much that you never make any progress. My best advice is to start as Steven Covey advices: with the end in mind.

Wisdom

- Do you want to be successful? Take action!

- Do you want to build a business? Take action!

- Do you want to be healthier and lose weight? Take action!

- Do you want to be wealthy? Take action!

- Do you want to author a book? Take action!

- Do you want to contribute to society in a positive manner? Take action!

- Do you want to learn a new skill or go to college? You must take action!

- Do you want a happier marriage and more stabilized home life? Guess what you need to do. Yes, take action!

As the Nike slogan instructs: Just do it!

Do what?

Take action!

What's the first action you need to take? Well, that depends on your personal situation, but you can't go wrong with dreaming. Dream your dream and dream it BIG or else you will cheat yourself. I assure you, I have accomplished everything I've ever decided to put on my goal list and after completion I always said, "I didn't dream big enough". Dream, then take calculated action.

Can you think of any worthy endeavor that does not require you to take action? I think not. The great thing about taking action is that the process continually provides feedback to help you move closer to achieving your desired goal, if your focus is locked in. Are you locked in? It also helps to increase your self-esteem, build your confidence, and enables you to shift the lens from which you view your life from that of a personalized lens to an objective lens. The more proactive you become in executing, the clearer you can observe your situation. Your focus should ideally shift from external elements and influences to internal precision and self-assuredness. If we neglect taking action when life is requiring it of us, we will encounter resistance, which will eventually lead to feelings such as regret and anger.

Five Truths about Taking Action

1. Success requires showing up.

You cannot expect any significant level of success in your life if you don't show up and take action. Have you ever watched a football game where no one showed up? How successful were they at winning? They who? No one showed up. Exactly! Have you ever had a clogged kitchen sink? How quickly can you get it fixed when no one shows up to fix it? You can't. I'm hopeful you get my point.

2. There are good habits, bad habits, and GREAT habits.

Taking action to achieve a positive result that improves your life is considered a great habit. A habit is nothing more than an acquired behavior that becomes an involuntary action, according to Merriam Webster dictionary. If you think about your own habits, how many require some form of action to take place? I venture to say all of them. From brushing your teeth, participating in a particular routine after work, to the meals you buy at the supermarket are all based on a habit that was formed over time. Even your shower routine! So how can you fast track your path to success? Consciously create the habits that will move you closer toward achieving your goals. Take consistent massive action and over time, life will smile on you with favor. This is how you create your desired future. Deliberate action.

3. *What delays or prevents someone from taking action?*

Doubt and Fear

"Don't let your throat tighten with fear. Take sips of breath all day and night before death closes her mouth". ~ Rumi

4. *Taking action disempowers resistance.*

According to Steve Pressfield in The War of Art, when you take action you kill off fear, doubt, procrastination, perfectionism, self-corruption, self-sabotage, self-deception, and the enemy within. You advance in life toward freedom. You are now creating your life. You are now worth a damn.

5. *Innovative thinking produces nothing without directed action.*

You have approximately 30,000 days on earth as a human. By the time you're 40 years old you're down to 15,000 days. W. Clement Stone reminds us that thinking will not overcome fear but action will. I encourage you to create some urgency about your life, especially if you've ever had a creative inclination in your body. If you've never had a creative thought, it's not too late. Louise Hay opened her publishing company at age 60. Ernestine Shepard started working out at age 56 and later became a bodybuilder. She's now 80 years old and still going strong. Even Nelson Mandela achieved greatness by being elected President of South Africa at the age of 77. On his 80th birthday he continued taking action in his life by marrying Graca Machal.

According to the Kellogg School of Management the average age of Nobel Prize winners and other great inventors is 39. So trust me when I tell you, you will be in great company when you choose to trust your intuition and take action. I'll leave you with this one question. What purpose do you serve if it's not to take some form of calculated action to advance society, even in the least ways of them all?

"Cemeteries are full of unfulfilled dreams", according to Steve Maraboli.
Don't let your grave be one of them.

19

The Superpower of Repetition

"Whatever we plant in our subconscious mind and nourish with repetition and emotion will one day become a reality."
~ *Earl Nightingale*

Repetition and repetition with a feedback loop are a couple of the best ways to hold yourself accountable for self-improvement. The mechanics of doing a thing over and over lends to familiarity, the law of averages, observable actions to later critique, and an opportunity to gain greater confidence in execution. Of all of these, the most important is the gift of familiarity; repetition allows execution of the action to become second nature. This is how great public speakers become great, great sportsmen become great, and great technicians become great. When your goal requires you to do something specific, it is in your best interest to do it as many times as possible to attain mastery over it. Start early, start fast, and start now!

Repetition is the secret to great vocalists because repetition is nothing more then continual practice. Who practices to become great? Everyone who achieves greatness. And they practice because the thing that they're doing needs to become a natural part of their daily lives; instinctual. Just like you get up and brush your teeth and take a shower, people who practice what they do repetitively consider it just as important as brushing their teeth and taking a shower. We can only get better at the thing we are attempting when we exert the focus and energy with direct intention for improvement. But never settle for mere improvement. Seek mastery! Dominate through repetition. Kobe Bryant was known to repeat the same basketball shot for hours while practicing in the gym without a tangible basketball in his hands. This helped him mentally master the action he was focused on perfecting.

Repetition has been called the mother of all learning. Initially, the repetition of an action makes it easier for the brain to remember the pattern of the thing you are practicing by mere exposure to your rehearsal of it. For example, research out of Cambridge University demonstrated that if you see a word 160 times in 14 minutes, your brain will remember it. We know that repetition increases memorization, habit creation, and mastery of skill. If we can create a repetitive process inside of a rhythmic motion, pleasure is increased, thus increasing the probability of future recollection because the fun factor increases a sense of pleasure, which is enabled by the feel-good chemicals (dopamine, etc.) released in the brain at the time of action.

Take for instance the increase in learning created by Dr. Seuss' songs, the military cadence, and rhythmic patterns in the beat of music, all which enhance the subconscious mind's acceptance of information. The learning pattern and memorization of the actions performed are all more easily repeatable because the rhythm of the event enhances the experience and encodes it in the mind.

But it's not just the rhythmic motion of the action that encodes it in the brain; it's also the emotion connected to the repetition. This contributes greatly to why smokers struggle to stop smoking. The rhythm of breathing-in repetitively creates a feel good emotional association to cigarettes and develops what we call a habit. Even after we decide we no longer want to partake in that habit, the emotional association has cemented the habit as a new neural connection. It's the rhythm that strengthened the repetition of the action that then became encoded in the mind. It takes great discipline to disrupt the learning, memory, and feeling associated with a behavior that has been cemented repetitively.

Repetition works the same way in relationships. People get used to seeing each other and accustomed to the patterns of interpersonal interactions so much that even if the relationship is unhealthy, it can take great efforts to break the habit of that relationship. The habit of being in a relationship with a person is strengthened by the creation of memories, which complicates disrupting the norm despite knowing it would be best for the parties involved. It can be difficult to change the behavior because it has been imprinted in the brain by repetition and emotions associated with the relationship. This is powerful stuff so it's important that you understand the power you possess. You have the power to not only learn but unlearn that which no longer serves your life's best interest. Work to master new information and behaviors that benefit your well being by using the power of repetition and then amplifying this ordinary power to a superpower by incorporating rhythm and emotional association.

How Memories are Formed

Neuroscience research informs us how the brain creates memory. According to Gretchen Schmelzer (2015), we must understand the basics of memory in order to understand learning and change. As information comes through our sensory organs (ears, eyes, mouth, etc.) information gets routed either through the emotional center of our brain or the memory storage center and then gets encoded in the brain. The brain then decides whether the information will stay in short-term or long term memory and this is based on the urgency, repetition, or association given to the information. According to this research study, urgency is solidified by the releasing of powerful stress hormones. If the encoding of the repetitive action is connected to a threatening element, which releases stress hormones, the memory can be stored in the unconscious center with an emotional rather than narrative marker.

Repetition creates long-term memory by eliciting strong chemical interactions at the connecting sector of the brain cells. Science shows that repetition is the only real option for learning, unlearning, and relearning. Yes, it takes time, focus, dedication, and repetitive action to learn or unlearn a behavior but this is exactly why athletes, musicians, vocalists, soldiers, models, hairstylists, and doctors repeat an action of their profession hundreds if not thousands of times before they are considered a master of their trade. Even the six-year-old learning to ride a bike must repeat the action repetitively until his subconscious brain goes on autopilot with this new learned behavior.

The Easiest Way to Learn Something

Repetition is the easiest learning tool to ensure memory of facts, words, and actionable behaviors irrespective of whether the behavior benefits or hinders your growth. This is your superpower! Why? Because now you are no longer just vaguely aware of the power of repetition, rather you are now acutely aware of the power of repetition. Additionally you're now aware of the neuroscience behind repetition and the realization that it is 100% within your control to use the action of repetition to change any area of your life and the science supports it.

How can you maximize the use of this superpower in your own life? Ask yourself, what do I need to get better at? Where do I lack self-confidence? What can I learn, or unlearn, using the power of repetition that would de-stress my day, increase my income, or benefit my future? Speaking of de-stressing your day, meditation is another activity that requires rhythmic repetition to master. Once you get the hang of focusing on the rhythm of your breathing, you will gain the ability to control your physiology and achieve the advantage of affect-regulation. The evidence based on habitual self-medicating vs. practicing meditation is a perfect example of how rhythmic repetition can completely change your life.

The main point to remember about repetition is that it's a tool for learning and improving your life. Isn't that what life is really about it anyway? We learn so we can grow and evolve. Repetition is also integral in helping us learn how to change our paradigms as evidenced by the rhythm of repeating mantras. As you can probably guess, the repetition of a mantra is amplified when it's applied in a rhythmic, emotional manner. Repetition increases our subconscious mind to its exposure and the emotion we associate to the mantra solidifies its encoding in the brain.

The mere thought that "I can do it" is only a reflection of the will but when continually repeated verbally in conjunction with that of the action desired to master, along with an emotional reason why it's important to master the action, then it becomes part of our paradigm. This is what happens when someone says "tell me I can't do something and I will prove you wrong". Proving their capabilities emotionally motivates them and turns mere repetition into a superpower by connecting that action to an emotion. These people will relentlessly repeat the action they need to achieve until they have proved their mastery, not by mere dedication but by emotional sustenance.

Mastery is enhanced when emotional repetition is utilized through mental visualization. Hence, Kobe Bryant won 5 NBA Championships because he tapped into his superpower.

20

The Superpower of Seeing Opportunity Everywhere

"Opportunity dances with those already on the dance floor."

~ H. Jackson Brown, Jr.

This happens to be one of my favorite mind hacks and if you can manage to retrain your brain to this perspective you will leave other people in the dust. It is 100% a learned perspective and it stems from the power of choice. Unfortunately, most people resist it vehemently. Why? Because neurologically we're not wired to find opportunity in every situation.

When you can see opportunity everywhere and in everything the world opens up to you. You will have, in essence, shifted your perspective to look for that which benefits you at all times. That goes against our nature of learned helplessness. But if you can train yourself in this manner, you will begin to maximize your influence over life as opposed to life dominating your psychology.

Will you take the lead over your life or will you find reasons to succumb to defeat and old patterns of thinking? Opportunity is nothing more than creative perspective. Aristotle reminded us that, "Nothing is good or bad but thinking makes it so". It is by your power of thinking, or lack thereof, that you will determine your own future. Will you entertain this possibility for a moment or will you immediately block it out due to fear and stubbornness. Fear and stubbornness thwart evolution. It's not always easy to be open-minded but it is beneficial. And even when there are times you honestly cannot find opportunity in a particular situation, especially a negative situation (which often is just

a perspective), at least you can say you were mature enough
to try.

The Tale of Two Men

Take for instance two men who experienced an identical
life event, which hurt them in some way. Maybe their wives
cheated on them, maybe they got fired, or maybe they had a
near-death experience. Now on the surface, these may
appear to be negative experiences, but what I want you to
see is it is a pivotal point that can lead to a new and better
opportunity. It is absolutely possible that one of these men
could become so devastated by such tragic events that he
succumbs to depression and becomes an alcoholic. It is also
absolutely possible that the other man goes through the
natural grieving process and comes out of it appreciating the
opportunity he experienced realizing that nothing lasts
forever. Change and death are the only things guaranteed in
life.

In order to not be overcome by what feels like a negative
experience, you must first BELIEVE it's possible to find

opportunity in what initially feels devastating. Let's examine the possibilities for the man who experienced devastating depression. Is his life over? Only he can decide. As long as he is still breathing, he has an opportunity to become an alchemist. How can this idea of finding opportunity in every situation help him in this instance? First, he must take the stance that he's not a victim, and shift into a perspective of personal power. The only thing he can control is himself, and more specifically, his mind. This is true for everyone, generally speaking. We all have the power to control our minds, which are informed by our emotions. We just need to learn how to do that.

The Mind

From the mind all things flow. A man can control his emotions by controlling his mind. He can control his behaviors by controlling his mind. This is the essence of thinking. When we control our minds, we control our thinking. We are wise not to let our emotions control our mind or our behaviors. Emotions surely will influence your physiology, but never let them control your results. If the man's mind has been trained to find opportunity in every situation, he can then see what most people perceive as negative as really a new opportunity. It's not always easy, but it is doable. The more deliberately we train ourselves to be opportunity seekers, the easier it becomes in difficult situations. What we're talking about here is being flexible in our thoughts.

Every situation in life provides a space for us to activate our creative nature. The man who gets fired from his job has two choices. One is to be devastated in his thinking. The other is to reframe the situation as an opportunity to move into a career he prefers that is more beneficial to his future growth and happiness. All too often people will stay in a job a relationship, or other situation despite their continued misery because they are wired to find the path of least resistance. Humans are notorious for turning a blind eye to what is glaring them in the face and it often takes a devastating experience to jolt them into a new reality. We are notorious for settling for what "is" despite knowing that what "is" is completely wrong or unhealthy for us.

A new situation, regardless of how it comes about, is always an opportunity to enhance our lives but it takes a keen mind to think in this way. It requires subjugating our instinct, our emotions, and all negative thinking. There are times when people can get very emotional, which often leads to fear dominating their thinking. Research shows that fear is generated from the amygdala, which is in the emotion center of the brain, and when fear activates, it can shut down operations in the prefrontal cortex where logical thinking occurs. But it is logic that talks us out of our pessimism, so we must learn the coping skills needed to reduce the fear so our thinking brain can come back on-line again.

Everything is a New Opportunity

Consider this: What if the tragic situation at hand could be viewed as an opportunity to "do" life better, to realize that life is precious, to challenge ourselves to dig deeper, and to find the warrior that lives within, or even to set our authentic selves free. Wouldn't you prefer this type of power over your life as opposed to letting life events control you emotionally? The truth is every situation is another opportunity for us to be better people, more patient, more compassionate, more forgiving, and more evolved in some way. If life did not throw us curveballs we could never develop into our fullest potential.

Complacency is also the enemy of evolution. When we are comfortable we take life for granted and life will not allow that. We live in a survival of the fittest world. It stimulates higher thinking capabilities because it challenges us to create new neuropathways in our brain. Without them, we eventually become extinct. Society, and life in general, is changing and advancing at leaps and bounds. Physics reminds us that everything is in a constant state of motion. How can we keep up with it? The answer is rooted in finding the opportunity in every situation regardless of how painful that situation initially feels.

Opportunity is everywhere. It's a lens from which to view situations in order to advance and excel despite initial emotional interpretation. If you can train yourself to be an opportunity seeker, you will surely be a happier and more successful person. Each tragic situation gives us an opportunity to become more resilient. We just have to decide to meet the challenge.

21

The Superpower of Having a Team

"Alone we can do so little, together we can do so much."
~ Helen Keller

Learning to design your destiny is an experience that will continually unfold throughout the years of your life. The exact destination is wherever you want to be. How do you get there? You get there by influencing its continual development in the direction you purposely pursue. As long as you have at least one goal you are designing your destiny and as long as you have one goal you will also need help. No one designs their destiny in a vacuum. That means no one can excel in life alone.

If by chance you're going it alone, as many people attempt, I'd like to take a moment to encourage you not to.

You're be wasting valuable time; you are causing unnecessary delay. The learning curve is often steep and life is just a lot easier when you have a team of people assisting you. Your team can be a team of one or a team of many. Only you can decide how many people you want helping you.

As I envision the future of my own destiny, I know I want a team consisting of at least the following:

- House keeper
- Personal assistant
- Personal Fashion designer (@jazmeup on IG)
- Personal shopper (@jazmeup on IG)
- Landscaper
- Make-up artist
- Hair stylist
- Financial advisor
- Photographer
- Audio/ Visual engineer
- Personal therapist

- Business coach

- CPA

- Editor

- Publisher

- Agent

- PR rep

- Webmaster

And that's just to name a few. Some are optional; some are not. I don't need them all at once but this is the team that I would like to start building in my own life so that I can focus better on designing my destiny rather than worrying about my house keeping, lawn maintenance, updating my website, or editing the books I author. We must know what lane we are best fit for and focus our energy on that. Imagine how much time I can save by having these other people on my team to assist me. I want you to start thinking the same way for your own life. Whatever you do, please do not start off by saying you can't afford to pay them. In fact, don't even worry about how you're going to pay them. Just create a list of people you would like to have on your personal team. You may even already have a few of them on your team. If so, keep building.

A Few of the Benefits

There are many great benefits to having a team of people helping you as you design your destiny, and again, your team could just include one or two extra people right now but the beauty of it is that with these team members you will most likely develop close relationships with many of them. Having healthy long-term relationships with people we trust is a prerequisite for a balanced and healthy life. So you see, it behooves you to start building your team.

Additionally, by virtue of these healthy relationships and by working together, you will be fostering deeper creativity and synergy amongst your team members, which will help complement everyone's energy. By challenging each others thought processes, you enable further growth and development, which results in achieving greater productivity towards the fulfillment of your destiny, and as a bonus, you get to enjoy the magic of collaboration. These benefits will open doors future opportunities that you alone probably would not have access to. They also cultivate a sense of accountability, reduce your work load, and any related stress, which enables you to focus more on what your destiny requires from you.

There's only so much one person can do by himself or herself. But when even one additional person assists you, you immediately benefit from a completely different visceral experience. Having the support, guidance, and care of another, whether on payroll or not, instantaneously reduces the possibility of experiencing depressive or isolated feelings that often accompany working alone. It is important to acknowledge that working alone has its benefits at times and should be a part of your weekly schedule. There is great value in alone time because we all need to gather our thoughts before, during, and after a project. This is especially true when planning out your workweek.

If you're a writer for instance, it's likely you value your alone time because that's how you protect your creative writing process. But, checking in with your editor, agent, and fellow writers once a month can fuel a real creative boost in your vision. If you are a small business owner, it can be a relief to have a collaborative partner to confide in and meet with for brainstorming sessions. So yes, we do need our alone time away from our team members periodically, but having a team on deck can also save you countless man-hours on a project and help you avoid spinning your wheels. Deadlines are better met and it feels great to have someone to celebrate your big and small wins with.

Some other people you may want on your team are:

- Spiritual advisor
- A virtual assistant
- A personal realtor
- A real estate lender
- An aesthetician

- A nail technician
- And eyebrow technician
- A couple of mentors online and in person
- A hypeman
- A communications coach
- A marketing expert
- A travel agent
- A personal trainer
- And of course, always have your BFF nearby

The list can include whoever you want on it and obviously you're not interacting with all of these people every day, but you want to have these people identified so you stay ready and don't have to get ready in the moment of need. Continue to build healthy rapport with them on an ongoing basis so they know they are your go-to-expert. Make them feel special. This way, when you need them they're more likely to make you a priority.

Be Purposeful Because You're a BOSS

Again don't make the mistake of going it alone in life. Be purposeful as you design your destiny; be purposeful about who is on your team and the fact that you're actually building a team for yourself. Yes, YOU! You are a BOSS! This is your life. This is your destiny you are creating. You are absolutely a boss. And every boss needs a team of people he or she can call on when in need.

Let the vision of your future be so electrifying and dynamic that you absolutely need at least one or two people to help you advance toward it. This is how magic happens. Magic does not happen while you're alone in your bedroom or living room playing video games all night. Have a real purpose for your future and get serious about it because one day, this gig called life will end, and what will your have to show for the decades you existed? Why not accomplish something amazing while you have the opportunity. There are no limits on what you can do, please understand that.

And having a team will help you accomplish your vision quicker.

Kobe had Shaq, Tiger Woods had his father, Mark Zuckerberg had his roommates, Batman had Robin, every athlete has not one but several coaches, Barack had Michelle, Steve Jobs had Steve Wozniak, and Warren Buffett has Charlie Munger, among many, many others who helped them build their destinies. Do not, I repeat, do not go it alone.

22

The Superpower of Annihilating Self-Doubt

"There is more than one voice in my head.
Everyday I annihilate it and everyday it returns."
~ Dr. Capri Cruz

There is a lot that can be said about self-doubt, such as we all experience it in some way, shape, or form for longer than we should. The differences in our results stem from who allows it to control them and who allows it to fuel their greatness.

Self-doubt is a manifestation of our own interpretation of events. Self-doubt is a compilation of thoughts based on our understanding of the situations we experience that then reflect back to us who we see ourselves as. These self-doubt educing thoughts beget additional self-doubt educing thoughts that then cyclically reinforce the premise of our self-doubt. It's a vicious cycle. These thoughts create emotions that confuse us and ultimately erode our own understanding of ourselves. So what is needed to break the unhealthy cycle of self-doubt? An interruption in our mental and behavioral patterns!

Here are my top four remedies to annihilating self-doubt:

1.   TAKE ACTION, MASSIVE ACTION!! Why, you ask. Because confidence comes from competency and competency by the act of doing. We can academize self-doubt and its bio-psycho-neuro-chemical effects all day long, but until we take action, its antidote cannot begin to work its magic. You cannot edify self-doubt away. You cannot pray it away. You cannot love it away. Yes, these elements can be a part of your self-supporting system, but the ONLY thing that annihilates self-doubt is ACTION! And a lot of it, CONSISTENTLY. Competency comes

through repetition. By sharpening your saw in this way, you gain confidence. You must level up and evolve.

2.   Okay, taking action absolutely is the ultimate answer for overcoming self-doubt but before we jump off the cliff and start taking calculated action, you must do and know a couple of things first. If action is the end-in-mind, you must begin with preparation!

First, you must start in your spirit. You must know who you are in Christ. If you don't know who you are, who you were created to be, and what God's Word declares over your life, then no matter what else you do you'll be doing it from a platform of sand, not titanium, and in time you will most likely sink. The power of self-doubt is not to be underestimated. It's far stronger than the power of the will because your will is ego driven. It has limited strength. Self-doubt, on the other hand, is a virus in your CPU (your mind) that seeps into your physiology to kill, steal, and destroy you and your future! It slowly creeps into your mind and spreads throughout your thoughts and then programs your physiological reactions through the chemicals produced by your brain. The only antidote for this enemy is God's Word and love, so it behooves you to know who you are in Christ in order to have the armament to fight your formidable opponent. This is an absolute game changer.

3.   Next, you must know how your brain and mind work. You are a spiritual being but you live in a human body. You must understand the difference between your brain and your mind. The journey you take to learn that will absolutely empower you over self-doubt because you'll learn about the mechanics of your own hardware (your central nervous system) and how it all works together to create and sustain this being called you. Don't take any shortcuts. Do your research. Read peer-reviewed neuroscience articles so that your knowledge base is a product of scientific research.

4.   My last suggestion to annihilate self-doubt is to make it your supreme goal to become financially wealthy and give away 90% of your wealth. Let me assure you, becoming financially wealthy has a way of annihilating self-doubt, especially when used to help improve and save the lives of others. If you need a reason, permission, or a rationalization

as to why becoming wealthy is a good idea, let it be because you realize that life is a game and part of winning the game of life is to be able to advance society in love, peace, security, health, wellness, etc. for future generations, which includes your own grandchildren. Become invested in that!

What greater purpose can we mere mortals have than to help those who don't have the resources or knowledge to help themselves? Money is just a tool but with the right tool you can create real change on earth as you simultaneously annihilate your self-doubt.

These four remedies to annihilating self-doubt create a win-win for you, your family, and society. Be Bold, be Great, or just be better tomorrow than you are today. As long as you keep moving toward your greatness, self-doubt will have no choice but to dissipate. It's not a zero-sum game because self-doubt never totally goes away, it only dissipates and becomes controlled by your awareness of it. It's kinda like fat cells. You're never going to be totally rid of fat cells but you can do all you can to reduce the amount that threatens your health by being aware of how they are produced and then killing them off with proper action.

As I conclude Volume 1 of Maximize Your Superpowers, my hope is that you can now see yourself and your potential in a more enhanced manner than you did before reading it. I hope these pillars of success aid you on your journey. They are the exact fundamentals that allowed me to go from being an abused victim of child abuse and neglect to becoming Dr. Cruz, an International Mental Health Therapist. They have been the building blocks upon which I created my own purposeful destiny. Take what serves you and leave what does not. You do not need to agree with everything I have put forth, but my hope is that you will at least be open-minded enough to consider how they might advance your life to its ultimate GREATNESS because you are worthy by virtue of being a child of the most-high God! It is your birthright!

23

Acknowledgements

Thank you God.

I now know the real *Secret*.

Just as my daughter is of me, I am of you, and therefore you
are in me just as I am in my daughter.

My power resides within me, not anywhere external of me
because in me is where you reside.

I am God in motion.

*Believe me when I say that I am in the Father and the Father
is in me; or at least believe on the evidence of the works
themselves.*
John 14:11

Made in the USA
Columbia, SC
18 August 2020